New Directions for
Higher Education

Martin Kramer and
Betsy Barefoot
CO-EDITORS-IN-CHIEF

Educating for Deliberative Democracy

Nancy L. Thomas

EDITOR

Number 152 • Winter 2010
Jossey-Bass
San Francisco

EDUCATING FOR DELIBERATIVE DEMOCRACY
Nancy L. Thomas
New Directions for Higher Education, no. 152
Martin Kramer, Betsy Barefoot, Co-Editors-in-Chief

Microfilm copies of issues and articles are available in 16mm and 35mm, as well as microfiche in 105mm, through University Microfilms Inc., 300 North Zeeb Road, Ann Arbor, MI 48106-1346.

NEW DIRECTIONS FOR HIGHER EDUCATION (ISSN 0271-0560, electronic ISSN 1536-0741) is part of The Jossey-Bass Higher and Adult Education Series and is published quarterly by Wiley Subscription Services, Inc., A Wiley Company, at Jossey-Bass, 989 Market Street, San Francisco, CA 94103-1741. Periodicals Postage Paid at San Francisco, California, and at additional mailing offices. POSTMASTER: Send address changes to New Directions for Higher Education, Jossey-Bass, 989 Market Street, San Francisco, CA 94103-1741.

New Directions for Higher Education is indexed in Current Index to Journals in Education (ERIC); Higher Education Abstracts.

SUBSCRIPTIONS cost $89 for individuals and $259 for institutions, agencies, and libraries. See ordering information page at end of journal.

EDITORIAL CORRESPONDENCE should be sent to the Co-Editors-in-Chief, Martin Kramer, 2807 Shasta Road, Berkeley, CA 94708-2011 and Judith Block McLaughlin, Harvard GSE, Gutman 435, Cambridge, MA 02138.

Cover photograph © Digital Vision

www.josseybass.com

CONTENTS

EDITOR'S NOTES

Nancy L. Thomas

What needs to be done to strengthen U.S. democracy, to make it work the way it should? Each generation of Americans asks some version of this question, but recently it is being asked with heightened urgency *and* hopefulness. Democracy is both a form of government and a culture, a set of values, habits, and skills that guide how citizens (used throughout this volume in the broadest, non-legalistic, way) interact to improve society. As a form of government, our political system's current characteristics seem to be vitriolic, unproductive, partisan discourse and a distrustful, frustrated, and divided public, of whom only a privileged minority typically participate in acts like voting or lobbying. As a culture, Americans separate along lines of political ideology, social identity, faith, geography, and class. These dynamics undermine vigorous public participation, a cornerstone of democracy, and prevent effective problem solving, which bode poorly for a society facing daunting political, economic, social, and environmental challenges.

At the same time, there are good reasons to be optimistic about how democracy can work. At the national level, expanding coalitions of civic organizations, scholars, public officials, and everyday citizens have generated a reform agenda and set of priorities that includes ethics and transparency in government, voter reform, collaborative governance, and expanded public engagement (Strengthening Our Nation's Democracy, 2009). At the local level, communities are experimenting with innovative approaches to public discourse and self-governance that are proving to be powerful antidotes to exclusion, disengagement, and political stalemates. At the heart of both the national and local efforts is a conviction that persistent public problems call for dialogue and deliberation that results in collective action by diverse groups of informed, skilled, motivated, and principled citizens—what many call *deliberative democracy*.

Strengthening democracy cannot be the responsibility of any one sector. It requires collaboration between private, civic, and government sectors. The purpose of this *New Directions* volume is to explore the role of one sector, higher education, in this democratic renewal work.

In these opening notes, I deviate from the traditional walk-through of authors' contributions. Instead, I weave descriptions of the chapters throughout a narrative on the characteristics, principles, and aspirations of a deliberative democracy.

One comment about language: I intentionally use the term "democratic" rather than "civic," not to suggest that one is more desirable than the other but as a way to clarify the scope of this volume. Democratic education is designed with an end in mind: a free society in which all citizens have an

NEW DIRECTIONS FOR HIGHER EDUCATION, no. 152, Winter 2010 © Wiley Periodicals, Inc.
Published online in Wiley Online Library (wileyonlinelibrary.com) • DOI: 10.1002/he.406

equal opportunity to participate in the social, political, and economic systems that affect their lives. Although civic engagement is undoubtedly designed toward the same end, it is broader because it can include apolitical learning and experiences. Democratic education is inherently political. It includes the study of systemic problems and contemporary controversies in society, their underlying values tensions, and possible solutions, as well as practical skill development and social agency—all connecting knowledge about and action to strengthen democracy.

What Is Deliberative Democracy?

"Deliberative democracy is a revolutionary political ideal," writes Harvard scholar Archon Fung, "[that] calls for fundamental changes in the bases of political decision-making, scope of those included in decision-making process, institutions that house these processes, and thus the very character of politics itself" (2005, p. 397). A deliberative democracy exhibits certain characteristics, primarily informed and motivated policy makers, experts, and everyday citizens working together to tackle public problems at the local, regional, and national levels. People examine an issue through a deliberative process in which they invite and consider dissenting perspectives, manage conflict, design solutions that are for the common good, and collaboratively implement change. Actions are taken with the understanding that, if they do not work, they can be reconsidered and adjusted. Policy makers are accountable to the public and explain the reasons for their decisions. This form of democracy requires not just a change in the way government works: it calls for a cultural shift.

Another way to explain deliberative democracy is by what it is not. Individual acts of voting, volunteering, donating money, writing an op-ed, speaking at a town meeting, adopting an at-risk child, and other forms of civic engagement are vital to our nation's civic health, but if they define the full range of citizen participation then we do not have a *deliberative* democracy. This vision of democracy can also be distinguished from what Jane Mansbridge described in 1983 as "adversary democracy," one characterized by adversarial competition between interests and a debate culture. One can argue that adversary democracy currently dominates American public life, reducing public decision making to point–counterpoint exchanges from which those with power prevail.

The ideals of deliberative democracy offer us a way to address some of the most pressing problems facing our nation today, problems that cannot be addressed by government alone or, for that matter, by citizens alone. "In essence," say McCoy and Scully (2002, p. 126) from Everyday Democracy, "the process should bring 'us' and 'them' together . . . so that the conversation is about 'all of us' making a difference in the community. This takes the focus away from 'this is what we hope *they* will do.'"

Understanding the Democratic Values

Advocates for deliberative democracy have no partisan agenda—the process is powerful because it invites all viewpoints on an issue—yet it is decidedly values-driven work. A legitimate deliberative process adheres to principles of inclusion, reason, neutrality, mutual respect, and collegiality[1]—values that both complement and conflict.

Consider, for example, *inclusion* and *reason*. *Inclusion* allows for broad expression of perspectives, interests, opinions, and new ideas. *Reason* suggests that participants learn the relevant facts and offer coherent, rational ideas. Reasonable people understand that dissent often produces insight and that perspectives should be open to new challenges (Young, 2000, p. 24), but do they feel the same way when faced with opinions and beliefs? Should expressions be limited to those that are commonly acceptable or justifiable for the greater good? Deliberation practitioners see passion, anger, and frustration as assets if they provide information about the intensity of participants' views, and they place less of an emphasis on reason than academic theorists do (Levine and Nierras, 2007, p. 14). Inclusion also implies equitable conditions for engagement, yet when everyday citizens discuss problems with policy makers and experts, who may have dedicated years to study an issue, are there ways to equalize the footing? Inclusion requires that people with power and privilege check their positional authority and historical advantages at the door, and that calls for a level of integrity and humility that may not come naturally. Even the term *inclusion* suggests continuing ownership by a dominant group with an invitation to others to participate.

The task, then, is to identify, discuss, and work through the values tensions. To do that, communities need to engage in a process of dialogue and deliberation that includes building a foundation of trust and interpersonal relationships. Listening is as important as talking, personal experiences matter, and the process reinforces the idea that real changes happen when they are citizen-driven (McCoy and Scully, 2002).

I usually distinguish between values that guide the engagement *process* and those that shape its *aims*. We can turn to the U.S. Constitution and its amendments not only for a description of government structures and procedures but for an articulation of what it means to live in a democracy, a society committed to ideals of liberty, justice, and equity. Fung, quoted above, offers a second reason why deliberative democracy is revolutionary: it requires "dramatically more egalitarian political, social, and economic conditions than exist in any contemporary society" (2005, pp. 397–398). This is not to say that Americans should wait until more equitable conditions for engagement have been established, particularly in light of recent reports that income inequality, by many measures, is now greater than it has been since the 1920s (Leonhardt, 2009). Instead, we need to be vigilant about the state of American democracy and actively *aiming* for an appropriate balance between individual freedoms and social equity and justice.

The academy is one of the primary institutions where people learn to work through thorny values conflicts. For this reason, this volume begins with a chapter by Peter Levine, who reviews the role of the humanities and social sciences in examining the tensions relating to *civility*. Restoring civility, he suggests, may require tradeoffs with other democratic values and could even lead to inequitable or unacceptably constrained discourse.

Cultivating Democratic Skills and Culture

Democracy, it is often said, is not something we have; it's something we do. Too many Americans lack the necessary skills for democratic engagement, and young people have fewer opportunities than prior generations had to learn and practice those skills. Schools, religious congregations, voluntary organizations, the workplace, families, and neighborhoods do not necessarily provide these opportunities anymore (Center for Information and Research on Civic Learning and Engagement [CIRCLE], 2010). Colleges and universities can provide students with distinct opportunities for practical skill building or they can identify democratic skills as learning outcomes for all students (in the same way that they might identify critical thinking or writing skills) and have faculty teach for their proficiency.

There is no universal agreement on *what skills* students ought to learn (anymore than there is universal agreement about what an exemplary liberal arts education looks like). Opinions vary (see CIRCLE, 2010; Colby and Sullivan, 2009; Association of American Colleges and Universities [AACU], 2007; Kirlin, 2003), but most share the following common elements:

- Effective communication skills (written and oral) in a variety of contexts and among diverse groups of people
- Effective dialogue, deliberation, public reasoning, and collaborative decision-making skills (e.g., critical thinking, openness, reflection, negotiation, conflict management, team work, organizing and leadership, consensus building, assessing and managing political dynamics)
- Competent understanding and critical analysis of knowledge and information (e.g., research skills, evaluating the quality of arguments)

Civic organizations might state these in more practical terms. Citizens should be able to come together and listen; ask questions; analyze and frame issues; make reasoned contributions; engage in intercultural dialogue on matters of race, faith, and class; invite and take seriously new or dissenting ideas; organize community engagement programs; match an issue or need with an approach to change; mediate conflict without oppressing people or views; and share responsibility for outcomes and actions.

One approach to democratic skill development is to have students engage in high-quality discussions about controversial public problems in the classroom. Not only will students learn more about the world, they can test and practice engagement skills. Doing so, however, raises questions for those who teach controversial issues. When should professors encourage discussion of controversial political issues? Should they disclose their personal viewpoints? In Chapter Two, Diana Hess and Lauren Gatti offer a practical framework for conceptualizing controversial political issues by distinguishing topics from issues and policy from constitutional questions. These distinctions are important to an analysis of how skillful professors facilitate discussions about matters of political consequence.

Some schools work to integrate democratic dialogue into the very fabric of campus culture. In 2007, the Ford Foundation awarded twenty-five colleges and universities grants to start "difficult dialogues" as a way to promote academic freedom and religious, cultural, and political pluralism on college and university campuses. Many grantees examined one issue or limited the program to the grant period, but Clark University set out to foster a culture of democratic dialogue campuswide. In Chapter Three, Sarah Buie and Walter Wright offer a case study of Clark University's Difficult Dialogues program, a comprehensive and *replicable* approach to developing a democratic campus culture by reforming curricula and student engagement opportunities.

Another approach is to offer courses specifically designed for skill development. The United States is arguably the most socially and religiously diverse nation in the world, and although that diversity is espoused as a great asset to a democracy, it can also divide citizens by where and how they live and what they value. This division is sometimes carried into campus settings. Nearly twenty years ago, faculty at the University of Michigan developed a program to address tensions resulting from racial and social differences on campus. Today, hundreds of campuses nationally support Intergroup Dialogue programs, and though the programs vary, most consist of for-credit courses in which diverse groups of students engage in peer-facilitated dialogues over the course of a semester. The research on their long-term effects is now coming in. In Chapter Four, Gretchen Lopez and Ximena Zúñiga describe the program and its achievements.

Democratic Education and Engagement for All

This generation of Americans not only has fewer opportunities to develop democratic skills, they have *unequal* opportunities to learn and practice these skills. People from low-income communities and of color are less likely to have opportunities to develop civic skills through schools or other settings than their more affluent, white peers (CIRCLE, 2010; Levinson, 2007). They are also less likely to participate in the political process. "More young people voted in the 2008 presidential election than in the 2000 election, and those voters were disproportionately well-educated," says Peter Levine, director of CIRCLE. Specifically, in 2008, 79 percent of young voters (aged eighteen to twenty nine) attended college. That same year, young people without college experience were almost half as likely to vote as those with college experience (36 percent vs. 62 percent). College graduates are also twice as likely to be active in community service (Kirby and Kawashima-Ginsberg, 2009).

Because of this gap in learning opportunities and the inherent political power gained from college-level learning, efforts to increase democratic education for college and university students are, paradoxically, likely to increase social stratification in American society, and this is an undemocratic outcome. The solution has to be a commitment on the part of the academy to provide opportunities for people to develop democratic skills, particularly in community spaces where they live and work, where public participation matters most.

In Chapter Five, Monica Herrera and Joyce Hoelting offer a case study of a multistate initiative to reduce rural poverty. The Horizons program was delivered through Cooperative Extension programs at land-grant universities in seven states in the Northwest. Their task was to provide training and coaching to strengthen community leadership and civic agency. Horizons also resulted in a reciprocal learning process that affected not just the community, but the very nature of some Extension programs. This case study has implications for programs in adult learning, offices of civic engagement, or community–university partnerships, not just Extension programs.

Another promising trend on college and university campuses is the development of centers, institutes, or programs that serve as hubs for deliberative work and local community problem solving. Some are linked primarily to academic disciplines; others are interdisciplinary. Many of these centers serve as "Public Policy Institutes" connected to the National Issues Forums network and the work of the Kettering Foundation, or are a part of the new University Network for Collaborative Governance. In Chapter Six, Martín Carcasson reviews the potential these centers have for democratic teaching, learning, and engagement.

A Research Agenda for Democracy

We then turn to higher education's research agenda. The academy does not seem to have any issue with democracy as the subject of scholarship, and indeed, deliberative democracy has been the subject of hundreds of academic books and articles, mostly in the disciplines of political science, philosophy, sociology, and communication. Many—Robert Putnam's *Bowling Alone* (2000), Gutmann and Thompson's *Democracy and Disagreement* (1996), Schoem and Hurtado's *Intergroup Dialogue* (2001), Eck's *A New Religious America* (2001), and Gastil and Levine's *The Deliberative Democracy Handbook* (2005)—are publicly relevant and catalytic. Others, such as

Stephen Macedo's *Deliberative Politics* (1999), raise valid questions about whether deliberative democracy is realistic or even desirable. Critical, theoretical analysis is worthy of more consideration, but it is not the point of this volume. Here, we challenge the role of academics as observers of democracy and suggest that higher education has a responsibility to do more.

I asked earlier, what will it take to make American democracy work the way it should? Scholars have a critical role to play by helping answer that question through research that is publicly relevant and designed to foster change in the way democracy works. Researchers have already learned a great deal about how to "embed" democratic principles and practices in public life (Deliberative Democracy Consortium, 2008, p. 1). They are open to academic–practitioner collaborations for identifying needs and developing research methodologies. This kind of research does not just study democracy; it practices democracy as a research method. In Chapter Seven, Kiran Cunningham and Matt Leighninger look at both the research agenda for democracy scholars and how action research methods can not only better engage citizens in tracking, measuring, and evaluating deliberative democracy, but further the goals of deliberative democracy itself.

Community engagement for the purposes of student learning, scholarship, citizen capacity building, or public problem solving needs to model the principles espoused in this volume; it needs to be democratic. Chapter Eight highlights the necessity for reciprocity, mutual benefit, and peer relationships in truly democratic partnerships between American universities and the communities that surround them. Author Byron White describes the dynamics of institutional power and offers suggestions for how colleges and universities can acknowledge and address these dynamics through structural changes and democratic practices.

Overcoming Barriers to Democratic Education and Engagement

This volume is premised on an optimistic assumption that higher education's commitment to democracy is genuine and thriving. Unfortunately, although nearly all colleges and universities can point to programs in civic learning and engagement, these are often diffuse, underfunded, linked to the hard work of a few people, accessed by a relatively small number of students, and disconnected from each other and from the institution's core curriculum. Does the academy have the political will, structure, or culture to be a part of efforts to revitalize democracy? In Chapter Nine, Albert Dzur provides a sober assessment of technocratic administrative cultures, ineffectual institutional governance habits, and professional norms of hyperspecialization that have led to institutional timidity and an implosion of mission and purpose at American colleges and universities. Colleges and universities will fall short of their potential for democratic education and engagement if they do not find ways to overcome these barriers. The final four chapters offer ideas for overcoming them while simultaneously advancing democratic education and engagement.

The academy periodically comes under public attack for political bias. The most recent and vociferous accusations are that the American professoriate is predominantly left-leaning and actively indoctrinating students with liberal ideology, as well as closed to anything but secular perspectives. As Albert Dzur noted in his chapter, the academy has become risk-averse and arguably "timid" about encouraging political or religious speech. Yet one point of this volume is that colleges and universities must be sites for the robust exchange of ideas, places where students, faculty, staff, and community members can engage in candid conversations about highly charged political issues. In Chapter Ten, I review these claims and the current state of academic freedom in an era of adversarial politics and culture wars.

Colleges and universities need to model democratic principles and practices in their governance and decision-making processes. Some institutions do address campus problems and make choices through an open process of dialogue and community engagement. Too many, however, do not. In Chapter Eleven, Bruce Mallory looks at shared governance and makes the case for infusing democratic principles and practices into institutional decision making, something he tested as provost of the University of New Hampshire.

Collectively, the authors in this volume provide a plethora of practical, replicable ideas for democratic education—what students need to know, value, and be able to do as citizens in a democracy—and engagement—how to serve as active participants in the democratic renewal work. There is more work to do, however. In the last chapter, I, with my co-author Matthew Hartley, outline a set of priorities for the academy with concrete recommendations for strategic action and next steps. By sharing these experiences and views, we hope that colleges and universities will reframe and align their existing programs and innovations with a vision for building a stronger, just, and deliberative democracy.

Note

1. This list reflects my synthesis of the work of democracy-builders such as Everyday Democracy, the Kettering Foundation, and Public Conversations Project, Daniel Yankelovich (1999) and some political theorists, such as Rawls (1998) (reason) and Young (2000) (inclusion and reason). Civic organizations rightly use more accessible language: "every voice matters," "listen," and "you can disagree but don't personalize" as ground rules for public deliberation. Gutmann and Thompson (1996), who advanced the term "deliberative democracy," identify as foundational principles of reciprocity, publicity, and accountability. I could have chosen, for example, "cooperation" rather than "collegiality," but I wanted to emphasize our *shared responsibility* for democracy.

References

Association of American Colleges and Universities, *College Learning for the New Global Century, 2007.* Retrieved January 7, 2011 from http://www.aacu.org/leap/docu ments/GlobalCentury_final.pdf.

Center for Information and Research on Civic Learning and Engagement. CIRCLE Fact Sheet, Federal Policy and Civic Skills. Medford, Mass.: The Center for Information and Research on Civic Learning and Engagement, 2010. Retrieved January 7, 2011, from http://www.civicyouth.org/PopUps/FactSheets/FS_10_Civic_Skills_final.pdf.

Colby, A., and Sullivan, W. "Strengthening the Foundations of Students' Excellence, Integrity, and Social Contribution." *Liberal Education,* 2009, 95(1), 22–29.

Deliberative Democracy Consortium. "Where Is Democracy Headed?" 2008. Retrieved July 12, 2010, from http://www.deliberative-democracy.net/index.php?option=com _docman&Itemid=92.

Eck, D. *A New Religious America.* San Francisco: Harper Collins, 2002.

Fung, A. "Deliberation before the Revolution." *Political Theory,* 2005, 33(2), 397–419.

Gastil, J., and Levine, P. (eds.) *The Deliberative Democracy Handbook.* Hoboken, N.J.: Wiley, 2005, pp. 3–19.

Gutmann, A., and Thompson, D. *Democracy and Disagreement.* Cambridge, Mass.: Harvard University Press, 1996.

Kirby, E. H., and Kawashima-Ginsberg, K. "The Youth Vote in 2008," CIRCLE Fact Sheet. Medford, Mass.: The Center for Information and Research on Civic Learning and Engagement, 2009. Retrieved January 7, 2011, from http://www.civicyouth.org/ PopUps/FactSheets/FS_youth_Voting_2008_updated_6.22.pdf.

Kirlin, M. *The Role of Civic Skills in Fostering Civic Engagement.* CIRCLE Working Paper No. 6. Medford, Mass.: The Center for Information and Research on Civic Learning and Engagement, 2003. Retrieved January 7, 2011, from http://www.civicyouth.org/ PopUps/WorkingPapers/WP06Kirlin.pdf.

Leonhardt, David. "Income Inequality," *New York Times.* August 21, 2009. Retrieved January 7, 2011, from http://topics.nytimes.com/top/reference/timestopics/subjects /i/income/income_inequality/index.html.

Levine, P., and Neirras, R. M. "Activists' Views of Deliberation." *Journal of Public Deliberation,* 2007, 3(1), Article 4.

Levinson, M. *The Civic Achievement Gap.* (CIRCLE Working Paper No. 51). Medford, Mass.: the Center for Information and Research on Civic Learning and Engagement. Retrieved January 7, 2011, from http://www.civicyouth.org/PopUps/WorkingPapers/ WP51Levinson.pdf.

Macedo, S. (ed.). *Deliberative Politics: Essays on Democracy and Disagreement.* New York: Oxford University Press, 1999.

Mansbridge, J. J. *Beyond Adversary Democracy.* Chicago: University of Chicago Press, 1983.

McCoy, M., and Scully, P. "Deliberative Dialogue to Expand Civic Engagement: What Kind of Talk Does Democracy Need?" *National Civic Review,* 2002, 91(2), 117–135.

Putnam, R. D. *Bowling Alone: The Collapse and Revival of American Community.* New York: Simon & Shuster, 2000.

Schoem, D., and Hurtado, S. *Intergroup Dialogue.* Ann Arbor: University of Michigan Press, 2001.

Strengthening Our Nation's Democracy (SOND). (2009). *Working Together to Strengthen Our Nation's Democracy: Ten Recommendations.* A report from a conference, August 2–4, 2009. Accessed November 8, 2010 at http://www.everyday-democracy.org/en/ Article.1059.aspx.

Young, I. M. *Inclusion and Democracy,* New York: Oxford University Press, 2000.

NANCY L. THOMAS *directs the Democracy Imperative at the University of New Hampshire and is a senior associate with Everyday Democracy.*

NEW DIRECTIONS FOR HIGHER EDUCATION • DOI: 10.1002/he

1

Incivility can obstruct constructive public discourse and problem solving. Restoring civility is a task for higher education, but it may require tradeoffs with other democratic values.

Teaching and Learning Civility

Peter Levine

Expressing concern over rampant incivility in public life is nothing new, but it seems to have exploded over the past ten to fifteen years. Pointing to a decline in national civility in 1996, Senator Sam Nunn and William J. Bennett, the former education secretary and drug czar, launched the National Commission on Civic Renewal. In his 1997 inaugural address, President Clinton called for "the politics of reconciliation." Law professor Stephen Carter's 1998 book *Civility: Manners, Morals, and the Etiquette of Democracy* became a best seller. Researchers track "the culture wars," divisions and disagreements among Americans (or at least their elected officials) based on political affiliation, class, race, religious faiths, and special interests. Television and radio talk hosts feed ratings by fueling fear and tension. In recent months, Tea Party protesters depicted as angry and uncivil have captured the media's fascinated attention. In May 2010, President Barack Obama told graduates at the University of Michigan, "The . . . way to keep our democracy healthy is to maintain a basic level of civility in our public debate."

According to a 2010 Allegheny College national survey by Daniel Shea, 95 percent of Americans believe that civility is important in politics. Most perceive that civility has declined, especially if they listen to the radio and/or pay close attention to politics, and 50 percent believe that there has been a decline in the tone of politics since Barack Obama was elected. Incivility is also perceived as a major problem outside of politics. In a 2001 national survey conducted by Public Agenda (New York), 79 percent of respondents said that "a lack of respect and courtesy is a serious problem for our society and we should try to address it." In the same poll, 88 percent said that they "often" or "sometimes" come across people who are rude and disrespectful; half as many said that they sometimes behaved that way (Farkas and Johnson, 2001). Political civility refers more specifically to norms of behavior among those who live in a democratic society. Political theorist John Rawls argues

New Directions for Higher Education, no. 152, Winter 2010 © Wiley Periodicals, Inc.
Published online in Wiley Online Library (wileyonlinelibrary.com) • DOI: 10.1002/he.407

Figure 1.1. Participation in Civic Activities.

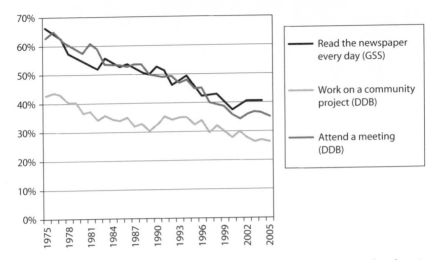

GSS = General Social Survey; DDB = DDB Needham Life Style Survey. Analysis by The Center for Information & Research on Civic Learning & Engagement

that political legitimacy must be based on public reason. "The ideal of citizenship imposes a moral, not a legal duty—the duty of civility—to be able to explain to one another . . . the principles and policies they advocate and vote for" (Rawls, 1993, p. 217). It means compromising, curtailing one's interests for the greater good. Defined this way, civility is a civic virtue. It is not the only civic virtue, and it can conflict with other virtues. It can also be defined in different ways by people of equally good will.

Civility itself is difficult to measure, but we know something about the frequency of public reason. Figure 1.1 shows the declining rates of attending meetings, reading newspapers, and participating in community projects in America.

As Robert Putnam (2000) has argued in his much discussed book, *Bowling Alone*, there has been a marked decline in almost every area of civic life, from political activism/engagement to the many forms of membership and local participation, such as parent–teacher organizations and neighborhood associations, activities that constitute the core of civil society. A major reason to be concerned about the state of such associations is the "normative concept of the deliberative public sphere understood as a core principle of civil society" (Cohen, 1999, p. 64). That is, statistics about the decline in associational life are troubling because we have a core value commitment to deliberation, and deliberation occurs primarily in associations.

The Opening Notes of this volume describe the promising new forms of democracy characterized by a high level of citizen (particularly youth) participation in productive, civil discourse. Recent deliberative experiments are not common or large enough to have reversed the national decline in civic engagement, but they do represent a base of concerned and active citizens who have struggled to enhance civility. In 2007, the National Conference on Citizenship asked a national sample of Americans whether "within the last year," they had "been involved in a meeting (either face-to-face or online) to determine ideas and solutions for problems" in their communities and whether that discussion included people who held views different from the respondent's own. The combination of these two questions yielded a group—18 percent of the whole sample, or more than 39 million Americans—who were involved in practical discussions with people of diverse views (National Conference on Citizenship, 2007).

Value Tensions Related to Civility

Civility is not a self-evident or transcendent good. It can promote fair, responsible, participatory democracy, but it can also trade off against other democratic values. Civility is welcomed by, and likely to benefit, some citizens more than others, and is likely to help in some situations more than others.

We know that various groups of Americans express different levels of concern for civility. According to Shea, women are more likely than men to define current politics as uncivil and are more likely to favor compromise. Currently, liberals are more likely to want elected officials to compromise, and conservatives are more likely to want them to "stand firm" (Shea, 2010). The ethical question is how to think about civility if promoting it would have asymmetrical effects. Scholars have argued that citizens who are reasonably well off and satisfied with the status quo are likely to favor civility (and to back out of politics or community affairs when things become uncivil). In contrast, advocates for disadvantaged populations explicitly say that deliberation is a waste of their limited resources (Levine and Nierras, 2007). They note that just because people are invited to talk as equals, the discussion will not necessarily be fair. Participants who have more education, social status, and allies may wield disproportionate power (Sanders, 1997). Individuals and groups who are satisfied with the status quo have an advantage over those who want change because they can use the discussion to delay decisions. (They can "filibuster.") Sometimes, the way the topic is defined can benefit one side over the other. If we meet to discuss the deficit, the conversation will favor fiscal conservatives, whereas if our topic is poverty, liberals will have an edge. When grievances are especially serious, it may be inappropriate to call for discussion among the opposing parties. For instance, the great African American anti-slavery campaigner Frederick Douglass simply refused to answer arguments in favor of slavery, understandably viewing the whole discussion as offensive (Sanders, 1997, p. 361). In the course of his nuanced and balanced study of civility as both an asset and a challenge to the Civil Rights Movement, William Chafe writes, "From a black point of view, of course, the ground rules, or 'civilities,' were often just a way of delaying action" (Chafe, 1981, p. 99).

Iris Marion Young lists some of the tactics that can be more effective than deliberation: "picketing, leafleting, guerilla theater, large and loud street demonstrations, sit-ins, and other forms of direct action, such as boycotts." As she notes, activists may even choose to "make noises outside when deliberation is supposedly taking place on the inside. Sometimes activists invade the houses of deliberation and disrupt their business by unfurling banners, throwing stink bombs, or running and shouting through the aisles" (Young, 2003). Here the ethical question is whether (and perhaps when) civility works for some and against others.

Talking with people who hold different views can cause us to temper or censor our sincere views to avoid confrontation, and such self-editing reduces our passion and our motivation to act. Diana Mutz has found that people are more likely to engage in politics (e.g., by voting) if they belong to politically homogeneous networks. When they interact with people who disagree, the pressure to be polite may cause them to suppress their own strong views, which depresses engagement (Mutz, 2006). Social movements that oppose injustice seem most likely to arise when there is regular and intense communication among people who share the same opinions (McAdam, McCarthy, Mayer, and Zald, 1996, p. 9). On a larger scale, election years marked by sharp political disagreements (e.g., 1968, 2004, 2008) often see high turnout. These findings suggest that the virtue and benefits of civility may trade off against the advantages of active social participation.

People of different genders, generations, race, ethnicity, national origin, and geography might disagree on what is and is not civil behavior and communication. Formality, directness, how freely people express their emotions, tone, volume, and inflection—these have cultural dimensions. Although the United States is one of the most diverse nations in the world, Americans are not in the habit of exploring their cultural communication styles before engaging in public deliberation and collaborative problem solving.

A final problem is that incivility can be good for business (or generally, for major institutions) even though it alienates citizens from public life. Diana Mutz and Byron Reeves exposed people to videotaped debates (conducted by actors) that were identical in substance—point by point— but that differed in civility. Viewers of the uncivil debates expressed considerably less trust in politicians and government after watching. Physiological instruments showed that they were emotionally aroused by what they saw. Viewers of the civil debate were less aroused and more positive toward the political system. Because the uncivil exchanges were more arousing, they make for better ratings (Mutz and Reeves, 2005). In contrast, the level of civility can be very high in facilitated deliberations that involve randomly selected, diverse participants. However, these events draw little public attention.

NEW DIRECTIONS FOR HIGHER EDUCATION • DOI: 10.1002/he

The Role of Scholarship and Teaching

The preceding section suggests that a society faces difficult strategic, ethical, and practical choices if it is concerned with the quality of public discourse and problem solving. Civility is one value that matters, but it is not the only value. It is important to understand the tradeoffs and tensions. One way for higher education to contribute is to provide research relevant to those strategic, ethical, and practical questions.

Some important research should come from the social sciences. For instance, we need more studies of the processes and conditions that promote civility, and the effects of civility on other aspects of democratic participation.

The humanities can also nourish deliberative democracy. They are the disciplines that most directly address contested questions of values, the same questions that animate public debates and divide citizens and their elected representatives. As scholarly disciplines, the humanities address these questions with a degree of detachment, reflection, open-mindedness, and collegiality—hallmarks of civility. The humanities first arose as the *studia humanitatis*, a curriculum designed for public life, and to prepare students for constructive participation in rhetoric and debate, not for contemplative lives (Levine, 1995, pp. 4–10; Levine, 1998, pp. 179–204; Levine, 2009, pp. 197–206). Yet the humanities have become relatively detached from public debates in recent decades and have not notably improved the quality of public dialogue. In a positivistic, science-oriented culture, questions of value are often understood as strictly empirical matters that ought to be resolved with data. Therefore, the scholars to whom citizens and policymakers turn for guidance are natural or social scientists, not humanists. However, empirical matters are usually inseparable from values questions, and failing to address values leaves them unexamined.

The humanities need a different relationship to public life before they can help to define and solve problems with our public discourse. Nevertheless, their potential is great and their preservation is essential for educating democratic citizens (e.g., Nussbaum, 2010).

Democratic education is most effective when students are asked to discuss controversial issues and conflicting values. Through an examination of civility, the humanities and social sciences offer students an opportunity for self-reflection and for living what Socrates called "the examined life." Students can learn to think critically about their habits, choices, and beliefs. They can practice reasoning together and navigating the inevitable conflicts over values that emerge in democratic life. They can develop understanding and empathy for those whose lives are differently or less privileged.

Civility and Local Engagement

It is important to understand institutions of higher education as more than gatherings of professors and students. They are also powerful organizations

NEW DIRECTIONS FOR HIGHER EDUCATION • DOI: 10.1002/he

with political and financial assets, distributed fairly evenly across our nation. The business of colleges and universities is the production and dissemination of knowledge both for and with citizens as well as the promotion of dialogue and debate. They provide an impressive infrastructure for those purposes.

Part of their responsibility is to provide literal spaces in which citizens can meet and talk. Campuses are often well positioned to host issue forums and to convene diverse community partners, with members of the campus community, for community problem solving. In doing so, they can serve as neutral facilitators who establish the tone for collaborative problem solving. It is in the context of setting that tone, in establishing guidelines for how people will engage with each other, that matters of civility, including intercultural perspectives and values tradeoffs, can become central to a public discussion. Campuses can organize ongoing community dialogues on the state of public discourse locally and nationally. They can host dialogues using already existing discussion guides, such as New England Center for Civic Life's guide (2008), *Responding to Hurtful Graffiti & Verbal Slurs: What Should We Do?* or Everyday Democracy's *Facing Racism in a Diverse Nation* (2008), both available through Everyday Democracy's Issue Guide Exchange.

Another appropriate role for local universities is to provide adult civic education. They can offer courses in the humanities and social sciences in which members of the community can engage in the same inquiries identified above. They can offer courses in technology, particularly social networking, blogs, and online political engagement, in which participants discuss how anonymity affects the quality of online engagement. They can study Constitutional principles, and balancing free speech and civility.

Colleges and universities can also provide professional development opportunities to teachers, particularly those who are interested in engaging their own students in discussions of the state of public discourse and whether civility for some is good for all. They can help teachers create their own political, but not partisan, spaces for democratic deliberation and learning.

The point of this chapter is *not* to denounce incivility or make the case for some universal code of behavior and speech. I am, however, advocating for more dialogue on the state of public discourse and on what civility is, who gets to define it, and whether it matters. I do believe that students should graduate with an understanding of what it means to challenge ideas strenuously without attacking people as individuals or as a member of a group. Learning and dialogue about civility is a learning tool, a means to an end, the end being more reasoned public engagement, a more inclusive and respectful public square, and a stronger democracy.

References

Carter, S. L. *Civility: Manners, Morals, and the Etiquette of Democracy.* New York: Harper Perennial, 1998.

Chafe, W. H. *Civilities and Civil Rights: Greensboro, North Carolina, and the Black Struggle for Freedom.* Oxford: Oxford University Press, 1981.

Cohen, J. L. "American Civil Society Talk." In R. M. Fullinwider (ed.), *Civil Society, Democracy, and Civic Renewal.* Lanham, Md.: Rowman & Littlefield, 1999.

Everyday Democracy. *Facing Racism in a Diverse Nation: A Guide for Public Dialogue and Problem Solving.* East Hartford, CT: Everyday Democracy. 2008. Retrieved January 13, 2011, at http://www.everyday-democracy.org/Exchange/Guide.13.aspx.

Farkas, S., and Johnson, J., with Duffett, A. and Collins, K. "Aggravating Circumstances: A Status Report on Rudeness in America." Public Agenda, 2001. Retrieved June 18, 2010, from http://www.publicagenda.org/reports/aggravating-circumstances.

Levine, P. *Nietzsche and the Modern Crisis of the Humanities.* Albany, N.Y.: SUNY Press, 1995.

Levine, P. *Living Without Philosophy: On Narrative, Rhetoric, and Morality.* Albany, N.Y.: SUNY Press, 1998.

Levine, P. *Reforming the Humanities: Literature and Ethics from Dante through Modern Times.* New York: Palgrave MacMillan, 2009.

Levine, P., and Nierras, R. M. "Activists' Views of Deliberation." *Journal of Public Deliberation,* 2007, 3(1), Article 4. Retrieved June 18, 2010, from http://services.bepress.com/jpd/vol3/iss1/art4.

McAdam, D., McCarthy, J. D., Mayer, N., and Zald, N. "Introduction: Opportunities, Mobilizing Structures, and Framing Processes—Toward A Synthetic, Comparative Perspective on Social Movements." In D. McAdam, J. D. McCarthy, and N. Zald (eds.), *Comparative Perspectives on Social Movements: Political Opportunities, Mobilizing Structures, and Cultural Framings.* Cambridge: Cambridge University Press, 1996.

Mutz, D. C. *Hearing the Other Side: Deliberative versus Participatory Democracy.* Cambridge: Cambridge University Press, 2006.

Mutz, D. C., and Reeves, B. "The New Videomalaise: Effects of Televised Incivility on Political Trust." *The American Political Science Review,* 99(1), 1–15.

National Conference on Citizenship. Deliberating. Retrieved June 18, 2010, from http://www.ncoc.net/index.php?tray=content&tid=top5&cid=262.

New England Center for Civic Life. *Responding to Hurtful Graffiti & Verbal Slurs: What Should We Do?* Rindge, NH: Franklin Pierce University. 2008. Retrieved January 13, 2011, at http://www.everyday-democracy.org/Exchange/Guide.41.aspx.

Nussbaum, M. *Not for Profit: Why Democracy Needs the Humanities.* Princeton, N.J.: Princeton University Press, 2010.

Putnam, R. D. *Bowling Alone: The Collapse and Revival of American Community.* New York: Simon & Shuster, 2000.

Rawls, J. *Political Liberalism.* New York: Columbia University Press, 1993.

Sanders, L. M. "Against Deliberation." *Political Theory,* 1997, 25(3), 247–376.

Shea, D. M. Nastiness, Name-calling & Negativity—The Allegheny College Survey of Civility and Compromise in American Politics. 2010. Retrieved June 19, 2010, from http://sitesmedia.s3.amazonaws.com/civility/files/2010/04/AlleghenyCollegeCivilityReport2010.pdf.

Young, I. M. "Activist Challenges to Deliberative Democracy." In J. S. Fishkin and P. Laslett (eds.), *Debating Deliberative Democracy.* Malden, Mass.: Blackwell, 2003.

PETER LEVINE *is director of Research and director of CIRCLE (Center for Information & Research on Civic Learning & Engagement) at Tufts University's Jonathan M. Tisch College of Citizenship and Public Service.*

NEW DIRECTIONS FOR HIGHER EDUCATION • DOI: 10.1002/he

2

Teaching university students through discussing controversial issues has the potential to build civic capacity and political tolerance.

Putting Politics Where It Belongs: In the Classroom

Diana Hess, Lauren Gatti

Throughout the last 50 years, the debate over engaging politics in the college classroom has raged on, sparked in part by the belief that liberal biases saturate scholarship and teaching in universities, which in turn lays the bedrock for the left-wing indoctrination of students. Polarizing and vitriolic debates abound regarding if, when, and how professors should disclose their political stances, whether or not they bear the responsibility to balance their curricular choices, and if and how they should approach teaching controversial issues. Frequently the pedagogical consequence of these debates has been to expunge politics from the classroom: politics are too dangerous, the thinking goes, too divisive for students and professors. In this chapter, we argue against this logic, asserting instead that politics indeed have a place in the classroom. Classrooms are rich sites for the discussion of controversial issues in large part because the students who populate them bring with them a diversity of perspectives, ideologies, and experiences. Classrooms can and should be places where students build deep knowledge about important controversies facing the body politic and where they learn how to talk and disagree about political controversies in ways that are inclusive and productive. When professors intentionally frame controversial issues, leverage diversity in the classroom, and are intentional (or not) about disclosing their own positions, they can facilitate rich controversial issues discussions in ways that work for student learning and democracy.

The rub for discussion-based teaching, however, is that its orchestration is as difficult as it is important. Many faculty members find it intimidating. C. Roland Christensen, who helped develop case-method teaching at Harvard University, described this kind of teacher as "planner, host, moderator, devil's advocate, fellow-student, and judge—a potentially confusing

New Directions for Higher Education, no. 152, Winter 2010 © Wiley Periodicals, Inc.
Published online in Wiley Online Library (wileyonlinelibrary.com) • DOI: 10.1002/he.408

set of roles" (Christensen, 1991, p. 16). He added, "Even the most seasoned group leader must be content with uncertainty, because discussion teaching is the art of managing spontaneity" (p. 16). Adding politics to the mix makes this form of teaching even more challenging because political discussion engages religion, social class, race and culture, power, and privilege—topics that have the potential to catalyze exchanges which cross a line from lively to destructive of relationships and classroom dynamics. In this chapter, we offer practical ways that professors can structure and facilitate rich discussions about controversial political issues without compromising relationships or learning outcomes.

As noted in the first chapter of this volume, communities across the nation are experimenting with promising forms of public problem solving characterized by high levels of citizen participation and carefully structured dialogue and deliberation. These well-designed processes require of citizens a number of skills, such as analysis, listening, intercultural communication, critical thinking, reasoning, and problem solving, all applied in a public and collaborative (as opposed to individual or private) setting. There is powerful empirical evidence that deliberation of political issues among a diverse public fosters learning. Several studies, many undertaken by political scientist James Fishkin (Fishkin and Farrar, 2005) on his "deliberative polling" process, examine fundamental questions about what results from political dialogue and deliberation, including the key question of whether political discourse is simply a communication strategy—the way one demonstrates verbally what one knows—or a knowledge-building act.

A deliberative poll is a process involving a random sample of adults who come together to engage in a structured deliberation about an authentic political issue (such as whether to close a school). This form of discourse is distinguishable from spontaneous conversations, which tend to attract people who already know one another and are like-minded. Deliberative polling, like most models of political deliberation, is committed to particular principles: political equality and inclusion (the consideration of everyone's preferences) and an open, public process of reasoning and deliberation (weighing competing arguments based on their merits). Organizers work in advance to research an issue and prepare background materials so that participants are *informed*. The sessions are moderated by trained facilitators who help the group establish guidelines for how they will talk with each other (e.g., respect, active listening), and experts are available to respond to participants' questions. Most of the deliberation occurs in small groups, and participants are formally surveyed about their views before and after the deliberation polling process. All of these components could readily be transferred to the classroom.

Research on the effects of deliberative polls that compares participants in polls with non-participants consistently produces the finding that deliberation catalyzes learning; this learning, in turn, shapes opinion. Frequently, people not only leave the deliberative polling experience significantly better informed, but also often leave having changed their views on the issue over which they deliberated (pre- and post-), which indicates that learning has taken place. Some follow-up studies show that these learning outcomes are long-lived: participants express interest in learning about the issue for months after the deliberative poll. This is significant on both individual and societal levels, for this intensified interest often inspires people to continue engaging the issue through pointed political action (Fishkin and Farrar, 2005).

In addition to learning and applying best practices in public deliberation to a classroom setting, professors must make other judgment calls about whether, when, and how to teach political controversies. One threshold question is how to frame an issue. When it comes to framing an issue, it is helpful to consider whether an issue is open, closed, or "tipping." Open questions are those for which we believe different answers could be legitimate. Though we may have personal opinions about the best answer to these questions, it is not appropriate to teach our students that a particular answer to an open problem is correct. Closed questions are those for which we believe there is a correct answer that we should teach students to build and believe, even though it may have been open in the past, or may even open in the future. What is considered open (and therefore, "legitimately" controversial in the classroom) and what is considered closed is a matter of social construction. Consequently, the same issue may be considered open or closed for discussion depending on the country, region, or individual. Just as questions are controversial in some places and not in others, over time issues can move from being closed to open and vice versa, a process I (D. Hess) have labeled "tipping" (Hess, 2009). For example, at one time the question of whether interracial marriage should be legal was considered controversial in the United States. Now the overwhelming majority of Americans support this civil right and it is hard to imagine much contemporary controversy about this issue in most university classes.

Before a professor engages his or her students in discussions of controversial issues, he or she should first identify if the issue is closed, open, or tipping. If it is closed, there is no need for discussion of controversial political issues, which is not to say that the issue should therefore be left out of the curriculum. For example, the issue of women's suffrage has tipped in the United States. Professors may teach about how women gained the franchise and why it was so important, but it is not currently a controversial issue. Nevertheless, teachers may engage their students in a structured discussion that asks them to deliberate the issue in the historical context. Issues that are "open" in contemporary society are the kinds of controversial political issues that are especially important to include in higher education classes. If the issue is tipping, there is also room for discussion, but professors should take into account the controversial nature of the issue while designing and implementing the curriculum, and recognize that the decision they make about whether to treat an issue as open or closed will undoubtedly be one that sparks some degree of controversy.

Much of the controversy that arises from teaching political issues emanates from professors' decisions about whether to present an issue that is in the process of tipping as open or closed. For example, in some university classes the issue of same-sex marriage is framed as open, and students are encouraged to deliberate it as a matter of legitimate contemporary controversy. But other professors treat the issue as closed and focus discussion on what can or should be done to ensure marriage equality. Not surprisingly, students are often not in agreement about how the issue has been framed by their professor.

Diversity and Tolerance

Teaching controversial issues through discussion strengthens democracy because of the causal relationship between discussion and the cultivation of tolerance. When we use the word tolerance, we are specifically referring to *political* tolerance, or the ability to extend basic rights (i.e., free speech) to those who are different from oneself. Fostering political tolerance is important for all democracies; however, in highly diverse democracies like the United States, it is particularly important that members of society cultivate this attribute.

Research shows us that political tolerance is best built through engaging in discussion with people who hold different opinions from your own. Diana Mutz's (2006) series of studies analyzing the impact of "cross-cutting political talk" on attitudes and actions is a particularly powerful one. Examining the "natural occurrence" of political talk within routine social life in the United States, she focused specifically on the consequences of being exposed to different political views than one's own. This category of talk—"cross-cutting"—allows Mutz to differentiate it from the talk people typically engage in, that is, talk with people who share similar views.

Mutz was certainly aware of the abundance of research that showed the powerful effects of highly structured deliberative experiments, like Fishkin's deliberative polling, but she was particularly interested in determining whether the same effects occur within the informal interactions people have within their social networks. Her core curiosity stemmed from a simple and important question: What are the benefits of hearing the other side of an issue? Although the percentage of people in the United States who engage in this cross-cutting political talk is low—23 percent—those who do engage actually become more politically tolerant. The connection between cross-cutting political talk and political tolerance emerges from two related reasons: cross-cutting political talk allows participants to become familiar with legitimate rationales for different, opposing viewpoints while it also legitimizes a political conflict. Mutz argues that this combination has important consequences for democracy because it often translates to the inclination to extend civil liberties to others, including groups whose political views one dislikes (p. 85).

The rationale for encouraging discussion in democracy as a way to foster political tolerance only matters, of course, if the health, stability, and sustainability of a democracy are bolstered by the extension of rights to those who are different from oneself. When a society lacks political tolerance, its enacted policies will likely deprive some groups of their right to influence the political agenda and to have an influence on decision-making. Consequently, there can be no political equality, and without political equality, democracies cannot flourish. This is one of the primary reasons why discussion in democracy and political tolerance are not just interrelated, but inextricably bound.

There is a strong line of research that shows that within the classroom, talking with people who hold different political views can similarly work to build political tolerance. One of the strongest studies illustrating this relationship between issues discussions (and other forms of conflictual pedagogy) and the development of tolerance is a study of 338 middle and high school students (Avery, Bird, Johnstone, Sullivan, and Thalhammer, 1992; Bickmore, 1993). Defining tolerance as "the willingness to extend civil liberties to groups with whom one disagrees," researchers created a four-week unit with a group of teachers that included a variety of active learning strategies, many of which centered on the relationship between the expression of freedom and controversial issues. Their research, which used a quasi-experimental design with experimental and control classes, found that most students, regardless of their gender, socioeconomic status, or previous levels of achievement in schools, shifted from mild intolerance to mild tolerance after the four-week curriculum. And these gains were far from ephemeral: a follow-up study conducted four weeks later showed that these gains persisted. Interestingly, however, a small group of students who demonstrated low levels of self-esteem and high levels of authoritarianism actually became less tolerant after engaging in this four-week, experimental curriculum. This is a disturbing backlash, to be sure, but it is not the norm for the students in the study, most of whom experienced increased tolerance.

Experienced differently by different students, the classroom is among the most complicated of social spaces. A majority of students might experience the discussion of controversial issues as engaging and relevant, whereas others might perceive them as uninteresting, or worse, as ways of creating or reifying unequal power relations among students in the classroom. Annette Hemmings' (2000) study relates to this latter point. In her study of discussion in two high school classrooms, she illustrates the ways in which sociocultural divisions shaped students' participation. Displays of tolerance, she found, sometimes actually work to mask deep race- and class-based divisions.

For professors who want to make discussions of controversial issues part of their pedagogy, Hemmings' (2000) research raises a troubling challenge, especially given the ways in which the belief that diversity is a deliberative asset underpins much of the theory on issues discussions (e.g. Gutmann, 1999; Parker, 2003). According to this logic, controversial issues discussions in a homogeneous classroom would yield less powerful results than would controversial issues discussions in a heterogeneous classroom where students come from different socioeconomic and sociocultural backgrounds. In a classroom situation where students are similarly situated, the thinking goes, there would not be enough variety in terms of opinion and experience to produce a meaningful consideration of competing perspectives. Simply put, it is less likely that discussion would allow students to develop respect for differing opinions if they are not given the opportunity to deliberate with diverse group members. Because the United States is a multicultural democracy, the classroom must mirror that diversity rather than concretize divisions based on religion, race, class, and so on. However, as Hemmings' study shows, although diversity has the potential to be a deliberative strength, it also can re-inscribe social divisions if students feel that they are being silenced during a discussion or do not want to express opinions that might be different from the majority.

There is no simple cure for these problems. However, research on effective discussion teaching points to some practices that are likely to mitigate these problems. First, it is important for professors to structure their courses so students know that they are expected to participate and when discussions will occur. Some professors expect that high-quality discussions will occur spontaneously as long as they have the flexibility to take up "teachable moments." This rarely happens in practice, in large part because we know there is a crucial link between preparation for discussion and high-quality participation. It is also crucial for professors to establish clear ground rules for discussion and explicitly teach the discussion skills their students need.

A mix of small and large group discussions can be especially helpful because some students are less comfortable speaking in large groups. Developing their skills and confidence in small groups can spur participation in large groups. Moreover, there is rarely enough airtime in large group discussions for all students to participate. However, small groups tend to have less diversity of opinion than large groups, so if one goal is to ensure that students encounter multiple and competing perspectives that cover a wide range, then it is likely this will occur more frequently in a large group. It is important to note that regardless of whether the students are working within large or small groups, there is difference to be mined. The challenge is figuring out ways to surface the difference that already inevitably exists in the classroom. Attending carefully to the design of questions and prompts is one important way to make sure that the underlying nuances of people's beliefs, attitudes, and opinions are surfaced.

Disclosing Personal Perspectives

Another major challenge for professors is making wise decisions about what role their own political views should play in discussions of controversial

NEW DIRECTIONS FOR HIGHER EDUCATION • DOI: 10.1002/he

political issues. Although some professors believe their own views make valuable contributions to their students' learning and have no qualms about freely sharing them, others hold their own views in check, either because they fear unduly influencing their students' views or because they believe it suppresses students' participation.

There is little empirical evidence from research on learning in higher education that would help us determine which of these stances holds the strongest warrant. However, a recent study of high school students (the vast majority in their senior year and thus only a matter of months away from our campuses) indicates that most students are open to hearing their teachers' views, and some see it as necessary for their learning. But they are especially wary and resentful of teachers who try to "push" their own views on students and are sharply critical of teachers who foster a climate in which competing views cannot be aired (McAvoy and Hess, 2010). Thus, professors should monitor carefully their students' views on whether they are interpreting the classroom climate as open to multiple perspectives and take that into consideration when deciding whether to voice their own positions.

Infusing higher education courses with rich and high-quality discussions of controversial political issues is not easy. In fact, what should be obvious from this chapter is that there are a number of challenges to this kind of teaching. The skill of the professor matters quite a bit; just as is the case with other forms of pedagogy, we know that few are "naturals." In fact, research on highly effective discussion teachers shows that they work hard to improve their practice, seek professional development on how to use discussion effectively, and continually assess not only what their students are learning from discussion, but whether they are becoming more effective discussants. For professors who make the effort to become skillful at this form of teaching, the pay-off is high. This kind of teaching can be enormously enjoyable and because the students are saying so much, it is also educative for the professor. The pay-offs for students are even greater.

References

Avery, P. G., Bird, K., Johnstone, S., Sullivan, J. L., and Thalhammer, K. "Exploring Political Tolerance with Adolescents." *Theory and Research in Social Education,* 1992, 20(4), 386–420.

Bickmore, K. "Learning Inclusion/Inclusion in learning: Citizenship Education for a Pluralistic Society." *Theory and Research in Social Education,* 1993, 21, 341–384.

Christensen, C. R. "Premises and Practices of Discussion Teaching." In C. R. Christensen, D. Garvin, and A. Sweet (eds.), *Education for Judgment: The Artistry of Discussion Leadership.* Boston, Mass.: Harvard Business School Press, 1991.

Fishkin, J., and Farrar, C. "Deliberative Polling." In J. Gastil and P. Levine (eds.), *The Deliberative Democracy Handbook.* San Francisco: Jossey-Bass, 2005.

Gutmann, A. *Democratic Education.* (2nd ed.) Princeton, N.J.: Princeton University Press, 1999.

Hemmings, A. "High School Democratic Dialogues: Possibilities for Praxis." *American Educational Research Journal,* 2000, 3(1), 67–91.

Hess, D. E. *Controversy in the Classroom: The Democratic Power of Discussion*. New York: Routledge, 2009.

McAvoy, P., and Hess, D. "Evidence, Ethics and Teacher Disclosure." Paper presented at the annual meeting of the American Educational Research Association, Denver, Colorado, April/May 2010.

Mutz, D. C. *Hearing the Other Side: Deliberative Versus Participatory Democracy*. New York: Cambridge University Press, 2006.

Parker, W.C. *Teaching Democracy: Unity and Diversity in Public Life*. New York: Teachers College Press, 2003.

DIANA HESS *is a professor of Social Studies Education in the Department of Curriculum & Instruction at the University of Wisconsin-Madison.*

LAUREN GATTI *is a doctoral candidate in the Department of Curriculum & Instruction at the University of Wisconsin-Madison.*

NEW DIRECTIONS FOR HIGHER EDUCATION • DOI: 10.1002/he

3

This initiative works to foster a culture of dialogue on the campus—raising awareness of discourse itself and encouraging skills and attitudes of responsible citizenship across our community.

The Difficult Dialogues Initiative at Clark University: A Case Study

Sarah Buie, Walter Wright

"I see my [Clark] education as split into two completely distinct halves—before and after dialogue," says Hannah Caruso, Class of 2009, New England native and passionate advocate for social justice, in describing her experience of the Dialogue Initiative. Similarly, Abhishek Raman, Class of 2009, a Tamil Brahman who as a child in Delhi witnessed Hindu–Muslim riots, came to Clark University (Worcester, Massachusetts) with deep questions about religion and intolerance and was changed by the work of dialogue. He said "I must confess that I landed on the practice of dialogue by accident and not by choice. But I wouldn't be the person I am today, and I wouldn't be where I am now, if it weren't for this accident." By their own accounts, these students' futures have been decisively shaped by the Difficult Dialogues Initiative.

For the last five years, the Higgins School of Humanities has worked to develop a culture of dialogue at Clark through our Difficult Dialogues Initiative. We know that genuine communication, creative collaboration, and effective problem solving are necessary to address the challenges we face as a nation and world; a renewed appreciation of democracy—its privileges, responsibilities, and necessary skills—is critical as well. Dialogue is a fundamental means for encouraging these capacities and insights. They further our abilities to work across difference, challenge assumptions, and develop new insights; they offer access to collective creativity and build momentum for effective action.

With strong faculty support and a $100,000 grant from the Ford Foundation (New York),[1] we launched the initiative in November 2006 after a yearlong planning phase. In our proposal to Ford we wrote that we would "examine and engender the kinds of dialogue critical to a vibrant educational environment, as well as to a democratic society." In this chapter,

New Directions for Higher Education, no. 152, Winter 2010 © Wiley Periodicals, Inc.
Published online in Wiley Online Library (wileyonlinelibrary.com) • DOI: 10.1002/he.409

27

we describe the core principles that animate our work and outline the range of activities by which we encourage this awareness and practice.

Core Principles and Intentions

Prevalent styles of discourse in both contemporary political and educational institutions have been failing us. Our politics are polarized, hijacked by cultural forces that threaten to paralyze the governance process. In addition, habitual forms of discourse in higher education do not encourage students to become engaged or to take responsibility; too often important issues are met with silence on campus. In approaching this situation, we followed three principles.

First, real communication and problem solving are imperative for sustaining democracy and our collective well-being. For those to be possible, we must become more conscious of our modes of discourse, and make new choices about how we speak and listen.

Second, unhelpful modes of discourse are often based on underlying structures that need to be made visible and evaluated. To shift how people engage with difficult issues, the "unnoticed rules of the system" must be brought into view. David Bohm (1996) shows that successful dialogue makes visible the assumptions embedded in thinking and speaking. Consequently, we chose to address our challenges with dialogue; we investigated it and introduced its practice throughout our community.

Third, we understand that we need to "be the change we seek." To foster an environment that challenges assumptions and creates intentional conversations, the project itself must do these things as well. Therefore, in developing and running the project, we encourage democratic processes that are open, participatory, and bottom up, hoping that the project itself can serve as a model for pedagogy, institutional governance, and practices of citizenship.

Multifaceted and emergent, the Difficult Dialogues Initiative has grown through the creative collaboration of faculty, staff, and students. It benefits from the remarkable commitment of many faculty, who have participated without reward or course releases. We initially encouraged interest and gathered ideas for the program through informal lunches with faculty and staff. A group of colleagues shaped these initial ideas into a formal proposal for Ford. Once launched, the project was centered in a small executive committee that, with the director, held the core of the work. A larger steering committee linked the ongoing work with the wider campus community.

The project has three aims: (1) to create a culture of dialogue by developing skills of dialogue across our campus; (2) to engage the community with the critical issues of our time, and to create opportunities for dialogue around these issues; and (3) to address the deep purposes of higher education, particularly critical thinking, creativity, and the skills and responsibilities of citizenship.

To prepare, we studied the theory and practice of dialogue, and created a reader from these materials. Studying the Public Conversations Project, Dialogos, David Bohm, Paolo Freire, Patricia Romney, and others, we discovered dialogue as a rich and complex concept and practice with specific dimensions that are often overlooked. At the first level, dialogue is an intentional conversation based on agreements that allow it to move beyond "discussion." Dialogue becomes a space of active civility around an issue by establishing agreements, laying groundwork for trust, and ensuring that each participant is heard.

Dialogue participants agree to share time, speak honestly, listen with respect, and acknowledge issues of power; they look to ask real questions and explore them with an intention to gain understanding; they agree to challenge their assumptions and listen for other possibilities; and they try to set aside fears and the need to "win." Experiencing this sort of dialogue is transformative, opening new possibilities that foster participants' capacity for democracy and civic engagement. As Abhishek describes it, "Dialogue has introduced me to the art of effective listening and the practice of respecting varied opinions and thoughts. It has taught me to dig deeper into my own understanding of the world by educating myself about how others see the world from their own lens."

Sometimes, in such conversations, deeper levels emerge. As people persist in dialogue, a dynamic, creative space can open between participants. In this openness, new understandings and solutions became available. Together with our principles and intentions, these deeper possibilities have animated our work.

Activities

From the beginning, we worked on many levels and in many venues of campus life. At the November 2006 launch, we asked, "What is dialogue, and why does it matter now?" "What are some of its methods, and its implications for the work of this university and higher education as a whole?" "Can we learn the practice of listening?" "What does it offer us?" The intensive two-week period featured a keynote by Diana Chapman Walsh (then President of Wellesley College); a panel with the Public Conversations project and Boston leaders on both sides of the abortion issue; a workshop on the Way of Council; and our first Day of Listening (a campuswide experiential workshop on skills of listening).

Our first efforts included four Difficult Dialogues (DD) symposia over the calendar year 2007. For six weeks, we explored (1) the state of our democracy, (2) race and ethnicity, (3) religion and tolerance, and (4) power. Speakers, panel discussions, workshops, arts events, films, Conversation Cafés, and Days of Listening brought a range of perspectives into play; we held dialogues at every opportunity, with many challenges to the participants' habits.

NEW DIRECTIONS FOR HIGHER EDUCATION • DOI: 10.1002/he

Hannah and Abhishek began their involvement with dialogue in the 2007 Dialogue Seminars. Caruso signed up initially because of her interest in religion. She writes, "The act of speaking out loud about my own experience and having people there to listen was very powerful. It allowed me to engage in my own development—personal, cognitive, and emotional. I began questioning things about myself that I had taken for granted. . . [now] I find myself asking a lot of questions about the assumptions we are making. I am more engaged . . ."

Abhishek describes his experience this way: "During the first meeting . . . [Sarah Buie] made us sit in a circle and explained the meaning of active listening and the acceptance of silence as a virtue. My initial reaction to the class was . . . skepticism; but at the end of the first session I felt my foundations being thoroughly contested. Why couldn't we just listen? Is simple attention so impossible? These were questions about me and my habits of understanding the world, which I had until then taken for granted."

With Hannah and Abhishek, as with many of our students, the experience of dialogue went deep. As the first two undergraduate Dialogue Fellows, they brought dialogue into many of their other activities. Abhishek incorporated dialogue into his roles as a Resident Advisor and as the President of the Undergraduate Student Council; he promoted interfaith dialogue on campus through the South Asian Student Association (SASA), and in his work after Clark with Diana Eck of the Harvard Pluralism Project.

Hannah took dialogue into her community organizing. Both served as effective co-facilitators of Dialogue Seminars and initiated a number of compelling public programs.

Building on its early explorations, DD has established a regular cycle of activities: faculty collaboration and development; a DD Symposium each semester—twelve to sixteen public events around a common theme; an average of sixteen courses each semester with a dialogue emphasis, with a monthly meeting among faculty teaching these courses; two Dialogue Seminars each semester based on the DD symposia and focusing on the practice of dialogue; the Difficult Dialogues Fellows Program in which more experienced students study, practice, and serve as facilitators in the Dialogue Seminars and symposium events, and bring dialogue to their peers in a variety of ways; regular collaborations with departments and organizations on and off campus; and outreach to, and consulting with, other institutions.

Each Dialogue Symposium addresses a critical issue with the intention of raising awareness of the topic across campus and in the Worcester community, and creating opportunities for dialogue around it. Programs offer information and perspectives, develop skills in dialogue, and encourage further action. Through Fall 2010, topics will have included Climate Change, Reclaiming the Common Wealth, Race in the Era of Obama, Old Forms Give Way/Visioning the New (Sustainability), Considering Gender, and Slowing in a Wired World.

NEW DIRECTIONS FOR HIGHER EDUCATION • DOI: 10.1002/he

The Symposium is also a platform for community outreach. In November of 2008, Hannah Caruso initiated a community-wide conversation on "what it means to be a neighbor" in a collaboration between the Worcester Human Rights Commission (where she served as an intern) and the Dialogue Initiative. This event was part of the Dialogue Symposium entitled, "Reclaiming the Common Wealth." After initial "sparks" (short talks or performances) from local musicians, poets, and other community members, 200 people—Worcester residents, public officials, community leaders, Clark students and faculty—sat together in small facilitated circles and discussed the question of "neighbors." This remarkable evening built on and deepened Clark's long history of community engagement.

We foster awareness of dialogic practices in community and student life by working with staff, residential and peer advisors, student leadership, and student organizations such as the Clark Sustainability Initiative (CSI), South Asian Students Association (SASA), and Hillel. Student participation beyond attendance at events or involvement in classes takes many forms, often with enthusiasm and commitment. Some are linked to particular issues—a Women of Color collective in IDCE, planning for Summer of Solutions by CSI, the development of a public dialogue event around the swastika symbol (SASA and Hillel), and the creation of a student dialogue group around the Israel–Palestine issue. Other students have taken dialogue practice to their work and study commitments. Still others have integrated dialogic practices in their student teaching, community service, and research and service projects abroad. For example, Hannah's experience with dialogue led her to volunteer with EPOCA (Ex-Prisoners Organizing for Community Advancement), drawn by dialogic "one-on-ones" between members of the group that are a core practice at EPOCA.

Clark cooperates with a wide range of organizations and institutes locally, and beyond. The dialogue initiative shares that spirit. In addition to the Worcester Office of Human Rights, we have worked with the Brookfield Institute, the Public Conversations Project, the NCDD (National Coalition for Dialogue and Deliberation), The Democracy Imperative, the Center for Dialogue at the School for International Training, and the Public Engagement Office at the Rhode Island School of Design, among others.

These collaborations include ongoing commitments to two particular issues. First, we address issues of the humanities and environment, local green economy, and sustainability in an ongoing way. Activities include public symposia (on climate change and sustainability), Dialogue Seminars, and support of student groups on campus, as well as leadership of the Humanities and Environment affinity group within CHCI (the International Consortium of Humanities Centers and Institutes). In November 2009, we sponsored a major community roundtable on local green economy that again drew 200 members of the Worcester communities for a two-hour dialogue across cultures of class, race, politics, and education. It brought together grassroots environmental activists, government officials, scholars, local nonprofits, business people, faculty, students, and staff. Following a talk by Omar Freilla (the innovative green activist from the Bronx), participants explored what "local," "green," and "economy" mean.

Our second ongoing issue is the Israeli–Palestinian conflict. This project has been an important proving ground for dialogue as a bridge across differences within the community. In response to a volatile exchange at a public event, Difficult Dialogues brought together seven community members involved in the incident and the topic. For two years, this group has studied, reflected, and sought greater understanding. In addition to its own conversations, the group has sponsored films, Conversation Cafés, community dialogues, public performances, and a student dialogue group on the issue.

Outreach and consultation have become a regular aspect of our work. From the beginning, the dialogue initiative attracted attention from a circle of neighboring colleges and universities. As we have grown, so too has the number of institutions seeking help in building dialogue on their campuses.

To help this growing community of institutions engaged in dialogue gather and gain visibility, we hosted a regional conference. "Inviting Dialogue/ renewing the deep purposes of higher education" took place in February 2010, with eighty participants from twenty-five colleges and universities, ten professional organizations, and twenty-five members of the Clark community. Diana Chapman Walsh (former President of Wellesley College, Wellesley, Massachusetts) framed the event, Patricia Romney gave the keynote, and Elizabeth Coleman (President of Bennington College) gave the lunch talk. Ideas and connections seeded at the conference continue to develop. In the summer of 2010, The Higgins School published *Inviting Dialogue/Renewing the Deep Purposes of Higher Education*. This document details our program activities, offers perspectives on the project, and suggests resources for others interested in developing such an initiative.

Where Are We Now?

The project's Ford Foundation funding ended two years ago (Spring 2008). Since then, the Clark Dialogue Initiative has been sustained through the Higgins School of Humanities and contributions from other offices; still, we continue to seek funding to ensure the continuity of the program. This spring (2010), with support from David Angel, Clark University's former provost and new president, we submitted an NEH Challenge Grant, which if successful could secure the project's financial future.

Meanwhile, on the Clark campus, awareness of the dialogue project and the concept of dialogue is widespread. A significant number of faculty and students actively participate in dialogue courses and programs (i.e., approximately 20 percent of the full-time faculty have taught at least one course with a dialogue emphasis). Public programs and Dialogue Seminars encourage conversations around the issues of race, religious difference, the state of our democracy, climate change, and sustainability. The Higgins School and the dialogue project continue to provide outstanding public programs, meaningful scholarship and pedagogy, strong design work, community involvement, and convivial hospitality. They offer resources for addressing many kinds of conflict.

Clark courses explore a wide range of pedagogical approaches including serious engagement with dialogue, and faculty remains excited about the challenges and rewards of this work. Substantial enlivened collegial relationships connect us in both informal and professional ways. We see more awareness of, and attention to, questions of discourse in our institutional leadership and faculty governance. Clark is perceived as an institution that facilitates spirited and committed engagement, in which we are taking up the challenges of our time through serious conversations. Our DD public programming has played a substantial role in creating this perception and reality.

At the same time, problems remain. We have succeeded in attracting significant participation in many of our events, but not all of them. Issues that test the limits of civility still arise on our campus. Faculty members face competing demands and even the most engaged are sometimes challenged to attend the full array of project meetings, teaching sessions, and events. Others are disinclined to consider these questions, through habit or lack of time, interest, or conviction. We are limited in our capacity to meet all the opportunities that arise to take our work into the community and the wider world. Despite some transformative efforts, the national political climate remains charged and stagnant. In our own community, we know that the capacity and willingness for dialogue cannot be taken for granted.

Nonetheless, students like Hannah and Abhishek exemplify the potential impact of this work and inspire its continuation. After participating in Dialogue Seminars and courses, many students ask faculty for classroom practices in which they can be more engaged and take responsibility for their own learning. The project has had an impact on the direction of some students' engagement while at Clark, and on the trajectory of their careers after Clark. After his work with the Harvard Divinity School's Pluralism Project, Abhishek has joined the Chicago-based Interfaith Youth Corps founded by Eboo Patel, where he is a Leadership Associate creating interfaith dialogue with fellows on more than twenty campuses. We see other students changing their career paths and making new commitments within service learning projects, internships, student teaching, and fellowships to work further with dialogue.

Our efforts have been aimed at shifting awareness, building skills, creating program opportunities, and integrating dialogue into courses. Through collaboration and conversation, we have encouraged many diverse environments for and we have worked to develop dialogue in larger contexts.

Nourishing each other, the influence of these experiences has spread in unexpected ways.

We see evidence that a culture of dialogue is becoming self-replenishing at Clark, an expanding web of possibilities and challenges, as it meets a yearning for dialogue latent in our community and our world. By cultivating suspension of one's assumptions, active listening, and respect for the voice of the other, dialogue is a fundamental means to sustaining civil society, creative problem solving and to bridging cultural difference.

"I think dialogue is incredibly challenging," says Hannah. "Just because I enjoy it doesn't mean it is easy. It is a constant challenge to step outside our habit of judging each other constantly and to refocus. To listen to others and try to actually hear what they are saying is not usual for us . . . . There are so many students from different backgrounds here. We are talking about those differences [in class]. Then we can go outside, beyond campus, and bridge the gap. We will be able to sit down with people all over the world and talk about our differences."

The benefits of dialogue make it one potent answer to the question of what higher education might offer in the way of skills and pathways to young people and to ourselves in these challenging times. As Abhishek Raman writes, "I am committed to bringing dialogue into every facet of my life because I believe in its capacity to positively affect the lives of those touched by it."

Note

1.   Clark was one of twenty-seven institutions among more than 700 applicants to receive full funding from Ford in March 2006. The Clark proposal was submitted jointly by the Higgins School of Humanities and the International Development, Community and Environment (IDCE) program.

References

Bohm, D. On Dialogue. New York: Routledge, 1996.
Buie, S., and others. Inviting Dialogue: Renewing the Deep Purposes of Higher Education. Worcester, Mass.: Higgins School of Humanities, 2010.

SARAH BUIE is director of the Alice Coonley Higgins School of Humanities and of the Difficult Dialogues Initiative at Clark. She is a professor in the Department of Visual and Performing Arts.

WALTER WRIGHT is associate provost and dean of the College at Clark and a member of the Executive Committee of the Difficult Dialogues Initiative. He is a professor in the Department of Philosophy.

Participants in intergroup dialogue examine the significance of social identities and social inequalities and practice intergroup communication and collaboration skills.

Intergroup Dialogue and Democratic Practice in Higher Education

Gretchen E. Lopez, Ximena Zúñiga

Academic communities must learn to address many of the social divisions, misunderstandings, and inequities of society as a whole. Although challenging, this offers tremendous opportunities for educators to develop, study, and learn from innovative programs that respond effectively to these social issues on college and university campuses. This knowledge may then be shared with our wider communities. This chapter introduces one such initiative, intergroup dialogue.

Intergroup dialogue is "a face-to-face facilitated learning experience that brings together students from different social identity groups over a sustained period of time to understand their commonalities and differences, examine the nature and impact of societal inequalities, and explore ways of working together toward greater equality and justice" (Zúñiga, Nagda, Chesler, and Cytron-Walker, 2007, p. 2). As examples, intergroup dialogues may bring together students (or faculty, staff) across race, gender, sexual orientation, social class, and religion- or faith-based divisions.

Intergroup dialogue represents an important approach for preparing students for multicultural democracy because it challenges students to grasp the significance of social identities and exercise critical imagination in understanding and taking action with others. Intergroup dialogue is distinct from other initiatives as it focuses on intergroup understanding and action while having students study and address the roots and consequences of structural inequalities. Through the practice of intergroup dialogue, students build experiential knowledge and leadership capacities for developing relationships across differences and conflicts, and for working collaboratively toward needed social change.

This learning and practice is significant from both the perspective of higher education leaders and current students. As examples, university

NEW DIRECTIONS FOR HIGHER EDUCATION, no. 152, Winter 2010 © Wiley Periodicals, Inc.
Published online in Wiley Online Library (wileyonlinelibrary.com) • DOI: 10.1002/he.410

and college presidents including Nancy Cantor (Syracuse University) and Beverly Daniel Tatum (Spelman College), also noted scholars on race and affirmative action, advocate for intergroup dialogue as a means to provide students with opportunities to practice engaging difference, and especially engaging difference within contemporary contexts of unequal power and privilege (Cantor, 2006, 2008; Tatum, 2007). Students also articulate the significance of learning through intergroup dialogue. One student, in an interview following an intergroup dialogue course, captured the need and importance of knowing and practicing the skill of active listening: "one of the biggest things that I took away . . . is active listening, which I don't think I really knew much about or did or practiced before this class." Another intergroup dialogue student wrote in a final paper about connecting newly acquired content knowledge with the need to take action: "This class has made me realize that I cannot be satisfied in just being educated on societal truths and realities. It is not enough to read about them, I must begin to actually do something about it."

Research studies further support this connection. Intergroup dialogue presents an important opportunity for students and others to practice the skills needed to cultivate diverse democratic culture in higher education and broader society.

Intergroup Dialogue: Academic Courses

Intergroup dialogue programs differ across institutions with each tailored to the specific needs of the campus, school, academic department, or student affairs unit that it serves. Undergraduate dialogue courses are generally offered for academic credit through Psychology, Sociology, Education, Social Work, American Culture, or other interdisciplinary programs or departments. The courses typically have twelve to eighteen students with fairly equal numbers of students from each of the social identity groups brought together through the dialogue course (based on student self-identification). Working toward this balance is helpful in acknowledging the historically unequal status across groups and the frequent unfair assumption of, or burden on, individual students representing (what is perceived as) the "whole group." Although intergroup dialogue courses are organized around a particular social issue and associated set of social identities, the pedagogy includes analysis of intersecting social identities and the heterogeneity and complexity of within-group, as well as between-group, difference. The design of the courses is informed by social psychological research on intergroup contact, as well as educational theory for democratic, critical, multicultural, and social justice education (Adams, 2007; Pettigrew, 1998; Zúñiga, Nagda, Chesler, and Cytron-Walker, 2007).

Undergraduate courses are co-led by two trained or experienced facilitators who identify with the social groups in the dialogue. On some campuses facilitators are undergraduate students (peers), on other campuses they are graduate students, and on still others they are faculty or student affairs staff (or combination). Facilitators generally work from a structured curriculum to guide the dialogue and are carefully selected, prepared, and mentored (Schoem and Hurtado, 2001; Zúñiga and others, 2007). Students complete weekly reading and weekly written reflections, a final paper, and a collaborative group project.

Educational Benefits for Students

The effectiveness of intergroup dialogue has been studied for some time, most recently through the Multiversity Intergroup Dialogue Research Project. This multi-institutional collaboration included researchers and practitioners—faculty, graduate students, administrators, and program staff—representing institutions with both longstanding and new intergroup dialogue courses. Participating institutions included Arizona State University, Occidental College, Syracuse University, University of California-San Diego, University of Maryland-College Park, University of Massachusetts-Amherst, University of Michigan-Ann Arbor, University of Texas-Austin, and University of Washington. This multidisciplinary team designed and implemented a common intergroup dialogue curriculum and researched educational benefits with funding over a three-year period from the Ford Foundation and W. T. Grant Foundation.

On each of the nine campuses, project collaborators offered two courses in conjunction with the study. One course focused on race and ethnicity and the other focused on gender. There were over 1400 participants, with approximately equal percentages of white women and white men, and women of color and men of color including African American, Latino/a, Asian American, Arab American, and Native American students. The study used a multimethod, longitudinal design to assess effects across educational institutions and educational impact over time. Collaborators collected quantitative data, survey data based on earlier research, and quali-tative data including students' final papers, videotaped class sessions, and individual student interviews.

On each campus, interested students submitted an application to take an intergroup dialogue course; from this pool students were randomly selected for placement into the courses or a waitlist control group (including over 700 students in each). The application and random assignment process addressed research concerns about self-selection; that is, the alternative argument that it is students' interest in gender or racial and ethnic issues that explains any change over time. The study further compared intergroup dialogue students to students in introductory social science courses. The results summarized here provide an overall picture of educational benefits based on quantitative survey results for dialogue and waitlist control students, and qualitative analysis of dialogue student final papers and interviews.

New Directions for Higher Education • DOI: 10.1002/he

Research efforts focused on three categories of expected educational outcomes: intergroup understanding, intergroup relationships, and intergroup collaboration (Nagda, Gurin, Sorensen, and Zúñiga, 2009). *Intergroup understanding* includes how students think about intergroup relations in the context of broader society, including students' awareness of structural causes of group inequalities. *Intergroup relationships* include affective and motivational aspects of group interactions, such as desire and ability to connect with individuals across groups through empathy (being aware and feeling connected to experiences, perspectives, and emotions of others) or bridging difference (sharing experiences and educating and learning about others). *Intergroup collaboration* captures students' engagement in individual and collective actions that address bias and challenge institutional discrimination.

Recent publications reporting survey results from the project offer strong support for intergroup dialogue having a positive effect for these educational outcomes. Comparing student change from the start to the end of the semester, intergroup dialogue students, when compared to waitlist control students, demonstrated significant change in awareness of group inequalities (intergroup understanding), empathy and motivation to bridge difference (intergroup relations), and frequency and confidence in taking action individually or with others (intergroup collaboration; Nagda and others, 2009). These findings are consistent with previous studies that reported positive effects of intergroup dialogue for students' awareness of group inequalities and action intentions (Lopez, Gurin, and Nagda, 1998; Nagda, Gurin, and Lopez, 2003). They are also consistent with previous studies on motivation to bridge difference and studies examining a broader set of democratic outcomes (Gurin, Nagda, and Lopez, 2004; Nagda, 2006; Nagda and Zúñiga, 2003). Further results demonstrate that a number of dialogue effects, based on longitudinal survey data, persist up to one year later (Sorensen, Nagda, Gurin, and Maxwell, 2009).

Other analyses delve deeper into these findings. For example, student participation in dialogue courses has been found to have an effect on students' understanding of the structural causes of racial and gender inequalities specifically (Lopez and Galbato, 2010; Lopez and Sorensen, 2009; Sorensen, 2010). This increase in structural analysis extends to understanding of poverty, even though the primary emphasis in the courses was on race or gender. These effects for intergroup dialogue, based on an overall summary measure of structural analysis of group inequalities, persist over time. Furthermore, structural analysis of group inequalities is associated with students' sense of efficacy for and post-college commitment to taking action. This is important because intergroup dialogue contributed to increased understanding of social problems while also motivating students to engage change.

Research based on individual interviews (248 students) provides further insight into how students reflect on learning through intergroup dialogue.

Qualitative analysis of the interviews identifies the importance for participants of learning about and practicing dialogic communication skills as a critical foundation for intergroup learning. Students' narratives identify listening to diverse peers' experiences as crucial in coming to a deeper understanding of power and privilege (Keehn, Mildred, Zúñiga, and DeJong, 2010). Listening to and learning from diverse peers, in addition to content-based learning, appears to help dialogue students develop multiple ways of making meaning of their experiences and observations. Additional results point to the importance of both verbal engagement and listening engagement for dialogue participants, and how the dynamic interplay between these two forms of student participation stimulate a range of reactions—cognitive, emotional, behavioral—and deeper forms of learning (Zúñiga, DeJong, and others, 2009). Further qualitative analysis highlights how dialogue students write and talk about action and future commitments including educating self, educating others, and working with others to create change on campus, the community, and social institutions (Zúñiga, Torres-Zickler, and others, 2009).

In sum, research findings lend strong support for the educational impact of intergroup dialogue courses in preparing students to engage differences while developing a richer understanding of complex social issues and imagining what is possible with a new sense of agency.

University–Community Connections

At both the University of Massachusetts-Amherst and Syracuse University, intergroup dialogue efforts are led through the School of Education. At the University of Massachusetts-Amherst, the Intergroup Dialogue (IGD) Program is part of the Social Justice Education masters program, which focuses on preparing reflective practitioners who can demonstrate competency in the knowledge, awareness, and skills needed to plan, implement, and evaluate effective education programs in kindergarten through twelfth grade and higher education settings. Graduate students enroll in a theory and practice course sequence, facilitating undergraduate dialogue courses in the second semester.

At Syracuse University, the program is administered through Cultural Foundations of Education with support from Academic Affairs and the Chancellor's Initiative Fund. Intergroup dialogue courses are cross-listed in Sociology and Women's and Gender Studies, meet the College of Arts and Sciences critical reflections requirement, and are open to students from across colleges at the university. The teaching team for the undergraduate courses includes faculty, graduate students, and student affairs administrators who meet together weekly throughout the semester.

The program efforts on these campuses link intergroup dialogue to broader institutional and community efforts. For example, Amherst College, Hampshire College, Mount Holyoke College, Smith College, and the

University of Massachusetts at Amherst partnered with the Social Justice Education Program at the University of Massachusetts at Amherst to implement the Five Colleges IGD Initiative. The initiative develops the capacity of faculty and staff to facilitate both one-time and sustained intergroup dialogues focused on race and ethnicity, gender, religion, and rank and class. A Five Colleges, Inc. IGD Training Institute was held in June 2009, with approximately sixty faculty and staff from across campuses learning dialogue facilitation skills. During the subsequent fall, "Days of Dialogue" were organized with each campus holding dialogue events on issues of race, gender, class, and religion. During spring 2010, a small group of faculty and staff interested in facilitating sustained efforts participated in five-week dialogues, followed by three-part dialogue facilitation training. The anticipated impact includes expanding the use of intergroup dialogue in the classroom and the workplace and providing students, faculty, and staff with shared language and skills for inhabiting and engaging increasingly diverse educational and community environments.

As another example, the program at Syracuse University partners with local high school teachers to offer a one-day institute on campus for eighty to ninety area students. These students have been involved in a teacher-initiated curriculum focusing on "race, rhetoric, and cultural voices" developed across two schools: one urban with an ethnically diverse student body, and one suburban with a predominantly white student body. The institute is organized around learning about dialogic communication, small group activities facilitated by university practitioners and graduate students, interactive presentations by faculty and staff, and student writing, analysis, and civic engagement. The focus during spring 2010 was "Raising Our Voices," including individually and collectively composed poems, connecting music and spoken word poetry, and planning group letters to advocate for educational or community change. The institute creates opportunity for teachers and students, university faculty, and graduate students to cross and blur school and community lines. The work requires institutions, as well as students, to meet the challenge of democratic practice and to experience its demands and promises in physical proximity with one another.

What these examples share, in design and aspiration, is capacity building for purposeful dialogic practices that can help develop a more democratic culture in higher education and our wider communities. These dialogues take place across different locations and involve faculty and staff, in addition to students. They support continuous and varied offerings and integrate the knowledge and skills of intergroup dialogue into new contexts, and educational and leadership roles.

Summary

As Beverly Tatum (2007) asserts, "Leadership in the twenty-first century not only requires the ability to think critically and speak and write effectively,

NEW DIRECTIONS FOR HIGHER EDUCATION • DOI: 10.1002/he

it also demands the ability to interact effectively with others from different backgrounds. The development of each of these abilities requires opportunities to practice" (p. 117).

Intergroup dialogues—and the institutional and student commitment and work that undergird them—may be challenging and time-intensive, but they are also clearly needed and effective. Research offers strong support for the promise of intergroup dialogue in preparing informed and engaged students and collaborative leaders. In sum, intergroup dialogue provides an important opportunity to develop and practice the understanding and collaboration needed to address social group divisions and inequalities in educational contexts and communities.

References

Adams, M. "Pedagogical frameworks for social justice education." In M. Adams, L. A. Bell, and P. Griffin (eds.), *Teaching for Diversity and Social Justice.* (2nd ed.) New York: Routledge, 2007.

Cantor, N. "Multiculturalism, Universalism, and the 21st Century Academy." Paper presented at the Future of Minority Studies (FMS) colloquium, Stanford University, Stanford, Calif., July 2006.

Cantor, N. "Candidates, Hear the Cry: "No Group Left Behind." *The Chronicle of Higher Education,* 2008, 55, A33.

Gurin, P., Nagda, B. A., and Lopez, G. E. "The Benefits of Diversity in Education for Democratic Citizenship." *Journal of Social Issues,* 2004, 60, 17–34.

Keehn, M., Mildred, J., Zúñiga, X., and DeJong, K. "Listening as a Pathway to Insight about Power and Privilege." Paper presented at the annual meeting of American Educational Research Association, Denver, May 2010.

Lopez, G. E., and Galbato, L. "Intergroup Dialogue and Students' Beliefs about Group Inequalities." Paper presented at the annual meeting of American Educational Research Association, Denver, May 2010.

Lopez, G. E., Gurin, P., and Nagda, B. A. "Education and Understanding Structural Causes for Group Inequalities." *Political Psychology,* 1998, 19, 305–329.

Lopez, G. E., and Sorensen, N. "Learning through Intergroup Dialogue: A Multi-University Study of Educational Outcomes and Processes." Symposium presented at the annual Teacher's College Winter Roundtable on Cultural Psychology and Education, Columbia University, New York, Feb 2008.

Nagda, B. A. "Breaking Barriers, Crossing Boundaries, Building Bridges: Communication Processes in Intergroup Dialogues." *Journal of Social Issues,* 2006, 62, 553–576.

Nagda, B. A., Gurin, P., and Lopez, G. E. "Transformative Pedagogy for Democracy and Social Justice." *Race, Ethnicity, and Education,* 2003, 6, 165–191.

Nagda, B. A., Gurin, P., Sorensen, N., & Zúñiga, X. (2009). "Evaluating Intergroup Dialogue: Engaging Diversity for Personal and Social Responsibility." *Diversity & Democracy, 12,* 4–6.

Nagda, B. A., and Zúñiga, X. "Fostering Meaningful Racial Engagement through Intergroup Dialogues." *Group Processes & Intergroup Relations, 2003, 6,* 111–128.

Pettigrew, T. F. "Intergroup Contact Theory." *Annual Review of Psychology,* 1998, 49, 65–85.

Schoem, D., and Hurtado, S. (eds.). Intergroup Dialogue: Deliberative Democracy in School, College, Community, and Workplace. Ann Arbor: University of Michigan Press, 2001.

Sorenson, N. "Thinking Structurally, So What? Implications for Action." Paper presented at the annual meeting of American Educational Research Association, Denver, May 2010.

Sorenson, N., Nagda, B. A., Gurin, P., and Maxwell, K. E. "Taking a 'Hands On' Approach to Diversity in Higher Education: A Critical-Dialogic Model for Effective Intergroup Interaction." *Analysis of Social Issues & Public Policy,* 2009, *9,* 3–35.

Tatum, B. D. *Can We Talk about Race? And Other Conversations in an Era of School Resegregation.* Boston: Beacon, 2007.

Zúñiga, X., DeJong, K., Keehn, M., Varghese, R., and Mildred, J. "Listening and Verbal Engagement Processes in Race and Gender Dialogues." Paper presented at the Northeastern Educational Research Association, Rocky Hill, Conn., Oct 2009.

Zúñiga, X., Nagda, B. A., Chesler, M., and Cytron-Walker, A. (eds.) *Intergroup Dialogue in Higher Education: Meaningful Learning about Social Justice.* ASHE-ERIC Higher Education Report, no. 32(4). San Francisco: Jossey-Bass, 2007.

Zúñiga, X., Torres-Zickler, A., Archer, S. A., Smith, T., Domingue, A. D., and Hopkins, L. "Exploring Student Skill Development in Intergroup Dialogues: A Qualitative Analysis." Paper presented at the Northeastern Educational Research Association, Rocky Hill, Conn., Oct 2009.

GRETCHEN E. LOPEZ *is assistant professor of Cultural Foundations of Education in the School of Education at Syracuse University.*

XIMENA ZÚÑIGA *is associate professor of Education, Social Justice Education at University of Massachusetts at Amherst.*

5

The Land Grant Extension at the University of Minnesota was part of "Horizons," a program using dialogue-to-action tools to address rural poverty.

"To Establish an Effective Community Spirit": A Land Grant Extension and Deliberative Dialogue

Monica Herrera, Joyce Hoelting

Background

In January 2003, the Northwest Area Foundation (NWAF) contacted land grant universities in Idaho, Iowa, Minnesota, South Dakota, North Dakota, Montana, and Washington to involve them in a program initiative to address rural poverty. After a strategic planning process, NWAF had shifted from traditional grant making to operating programs that address poverty. One program was called *Horizons*. Its goal was to nurture rural leadership and mobilize local energy to address poverty.

To Cooperative Extension leaders, the prospect of delivering the program was both exciting and daunting. On one hand, the initiative's goals made good use of Extension's relationships with rural communities and spoke to Extension's historic charge. In 1909, Theodore Roosevelt's Commission on Country Life described the goal for Extension this way: "It is to the Extension department of [the land grant] colleges . . . that we must now look for the most effective rousing of the people on the land . . . . It is of the greatest consequence that the people of the open country should learn to work together, not only for the purpose of forwarding their economic interests and of competing with other men who are organizing, but also to develop themselves and to establish an effective community spirit" (Commission on Country Life, 1909).

With that charge, Extension rooted itself deeply in "educational organizing that develops civic leadership skills and capacities, and builds respectful, reciprocal relationships between universities and communities through

NEW DIRECTIONS FOR HIGHER EDUCATION, no. 152, Winter 2010 © Wiley Periodicals, Inc.
Published online in Wiley Online Library (wileyonlinelibrary.com) • DOI: 10.1002/he.411

concrete public work" (Peters, 2002). Historically, Extension faculty research public problems and deliver educational programs that help rural communities create solutions and take advantage of opportunities. For example, Extension has helped communities address rural electrification, mobilize market cooperatives, fight hog cholera, and survive economic farm crises.

But poverty? With notable exceptions (financial literacy, farmer debt mediation programs, and others), Extension has not played a prominent role as a social service or advocacy organization regarding rural poverty.

Seven years later, Extension has met the challenge. *Horizons* mobilized everyday people in Minnesota communities to work together to address poverty. For the University of Minnesota Extension (UMN Extension), the initiative created an illuminating experience in using deliberative dialogue as a tool for poverty reduction.

Program Framework

When *Horizons* began, the NWAF had already made some key design decisions about the *Horizons* program. *Horizons* would engage communities under 5,000 in population. Very small communities often have limited government services and diminished access to nonprofit organizations. The delivery organizations (institutions that would implement *Horizons* in each state) would test common curricula and program components so that the cause and effect of their intervention could be measured. Extension programs would provide intensive community coaching by facilitating community action through *Horizons* program components.

The NWAF also decided to test the concept of "tipping point" in rural communities. Based on the work of Malcolm Gladwell (2000), NWAF wondered whether a viral effect might take hold if communities were pushed to involve at least 15 percent of their population in a new vision for prosperity. Their goal was to reach 300 to 400 communities by 2008 and involve at least 15 percent of each community—a daunting task for the delivery organizations selected to do the work.

Selecting the Delivery Organizations

The NWAF sought delivery organizations that could work with many communities both during and after the grant period. The NWAF's initial criteria included (1) positive, or at least neutral, relationships with rural communities; (2) the ability to work statewide; (3) the ability and desire to work across community demographics, including low-income populations; (4) a commitment or willingness to take on the issue of poverty; (5) the ability to work with communities over a long period; and (6) strong management and financial systems. NWAF then narrowed the criteria to organizations that had programming breadth and depth, a solid track record of management and fiscal accountability, and good working relationships in their states. They also wanted organizations that could work together to contribute to program design, implementation, and evaluation. Eventually, NWAF selected six land grant universities' Extension programs and one tribal college. As grantees, their directive was to assist in program design, guide communities through program implementation, and provide education that would build the capacity of everyday citizens in *Horizons* communities to create local change. At about that same time, community development efforts at UMN Extension were moving from the fringe of Extension work to a new Center for Community Vitality—with leadership, staff, and a mission to create vital communities. The Center wanted to build upon decades of well-respected, yet disconnected Extension efforts to strengthen leadership, design public participation strategies, and support community business climates. The new center created ties to the Department of Applied Economics, the Humphrey Institute of Public Affairs, and the College of Design. Its staff had degrees and expertise in subjects such as community leadership, economics, public policy, adult education, and community psychology. This organizational home for *Horizons* provided scholarship, statewide influence, and partnerships in the field of community development that could bring additional resources to community needs (Morse, 2009).

Lessons from the Pilot Phase

As *Horizons* partners convened, the Foundation and delivery organizations reconciled past programming structures with the goals of the new endeavor. Four program anchors drove program operations: (1) leadership development, (2) a poverty focus, (3) community development, and (4) collaborative governance. Four principles guided the work: (1) include everyone, (2) learn through sharing, (3) welcome change, and (4) sustain hope.

UMN Extension selected three pilot communities in fall 2003. The eighteen-month pilot included leadership education (utilizing the LeadershipPlenty® curriculum; Pew Partnership for Civic Change, 2007), visioning, and community action planning to help communities establish a broader and deeper leader base, and where necessary, new structures. As is common in pilot projects, however, the new program struggled with clarity in program intention. Evaluations of the first *Horizons* cohort showed that community members were unclear how to incorporate poverty reduction into their vision, goals, and planning. The design team realized the program had skipped an important step. *Horizons* participants in the first iteration had not come to a common understanding of the conditions, causes, and implications of poverty.

Adding Community Dialogue to the Program Design

The NWAF recruited Everyday Democracy (then Study Circles Resource Center) to introduce into the program a community dialogue component that could lead to embedded deliberative practices. Everyday Democracy provided technical advice and support for the study circles component of the overall program, conducting community organizing and facilitator trainings with and for Extension staff. They also developed, in collaboration with Extension staff, a discussion guide to help community participants study and talk about poverty. The resulting guide, *Thriving Communities: Working Together to Move from Poverty to Prosperity for All*, served as a common basis for dialogues—what we called "study circles"—in *Horizons* communities.

The progression of the dialogue outlined in *Thriving Communities* is a typical study circles process. Dialogues are led by community members who have been specially trained as facilitators. The circles usually consisted of eight to twelve people who agreed to meet for six, two-hour sessions over a specific period (anywhere from six to ten weeks). Communities convened multiple circles concurrently to meet the minimum participation threshold required in the program (minimum participant number was thirty and then increased with community population). The sessions followed a progression that started with the exchange of personal stories before moving to a discussion of the nature of the problem.

Although groups typically want to jump to action in the first meeting, the process is designed to temper those instincts and force participants to think carefully about the underlying conditions that cause poverty; what individuals, civic organizations, or government agencies are doing to address it; and what the community could look like if the problems associated with poverty did not exist. It is only after the process of study and reflection that circle participants started brainstorming action strategies. By then, they had built trust and a spirit of collaboration—two characteristics that carried them long after the dialogues concluded. Once all of the circles had been completed, the communities came together in an "action forum" where circle participants could see the ideas generated in different groups and like-minded ideas and people could explore ways to work together.

It was not a seamless "fit" between these newly introduced processes and the way Extension approached community work. Extension and Everyday Democracy shared beliefs in civic engagement, community development practices, and building local skills and capacity. However, the Extension's main orientation was to act as primary deliverers of educational programming. "Stepping back" to let peer facilitators lead the process and implement change was a challenge. Moving to a position of coaching and support required Extension to check some of their positional authority at the door.

Making the program fit was also complicated because each Extension delivery organization in *Horizons* states had different structural, staffing, and stakeholder considerations that affected their response to the challenge. Nomenclature was also a problem, as each *Horizons* partner engaged in the discussion with their own interpretation of what constituted "civic engagement" vis-á-vis "deliberative democracy."

NEW DIRECTIONS FOR HIGHER EDUCATION • DOI: 10.1002/he

Through their work with the design team and Everyday Democracy, Extension discovered new ways to apply expertise in communities. Specifically, the processes helped communities define their own needs and action ideas and then request resources they needed to achieve their vision for success.

In Minnesota's experience, many Extension staff fit easily into the new role. Others saw this as the "way of the future" for community work in an era when information is more accessible and collaborative, locally citizen-driven community change is a growing ideal. Still, the *Horizons* program had a different directive than other Center for Community Vitality programs, and roles between the program and Extension had to be negotiated. Ultimately, *Horizons* provided UMN Extension the opportunity to play different roles in communities over time—as facilitators, educators, partners, and learners. Sometimes, Extension's structured programs were challenged when community members found their voice through the public dialogue process. This created a challenging reciprocal relationship as communities became more active partners in, rather than just consumers of, research and education.

After seeing the effects of *Thriving Communities* dialogues when they were added to the second *Horizons* cohort, Extension staff gained insight into the power of dialogue. Bringing community members together to talk about poverty seemed, at the beginning of the project, unrealistic. "When we were mocking up fliers to recruit people to the program," said one program administrator, "I couldn't figure out what would motivate people to give up their Wednesday nights to go to a room and talk out loud about something that causes most people to whisper."

But it wasn't as hard as originally thought. "People showed up," says Donna Rae Scheffert, a retired UMN Extension leadership education specialist who helped design the program. "The curriculum talks about poverty, but it also gets people thinking about a vision for prosperity. The conversations gave people the chance to act on the desire to create a better place for the next generation."

A key to successful recruitment was local organizing. In one town, two Latino teenagers became *Thriving Communities* facilitators. Deeply committed to poverty issues, they used this opportunity to recruit youth to discuss poverty at their high school. These youth groups developed a ground rule that conversations would be held in both Spanish and English. (They introduced this ground rule to community action forums, as well.) Observing this, Extension saw the benefit of local ownership: it fostered more diverse participation.

Ultimately, Extension staff embraced dialogue as a way to manage difficult topics. The *Thriving Communities* dialogues made participants more aware of who lived in their communities and of biases that created impositions in others' lives. For example, after one participant said, "We should just bulldoze (that trailer court). It's a blight," a second participant responded, "I hope you don't. My son and I live there."

Talking about poverty is hard. Bigotry and isolationism surfaced. Some people in *Horizons* communities were hurt by comments made in the circles. Nevertheless, as the groups worked through conflicts, they developed more trusting relationships and respectful environments. No one walked away from the experience without a broader feeling of who "we" were as a community with poverty in its midst.

Most importantly, people became passionate about working together to make change. This passion, because it was fueled by leadership education and support for action planning, created successful community initiatives. Participants created food shelves. They published resource guides. They formed pastoral committees and started a community foundation. Leaders and educators involved with the program got excited about how *Horizons* could impact the future of both communities and the Extension.

Institutional Impacts

In Minnesota, *Horizons* brought change to the programs, research, and roles the Center for Community Vitality brought to communities. For example, some Extension educators began to integrate dialogue about rural poverty into other leadership education programs, stimulating discussion that challenged rural leaders to see that poverty does not only happen in urban areas.

The Center has used its Horizons experience to contribute new research to the field of community development. In 2007, the Center set out to examine the topic of community readiness. Researchers studied the nine *Horizons* communities. They examined whether and how trust and reciprocity increases program success. From that, they developed a community readiness assessment to help community development professionals examine local connections, networks, and trust before introducing community initiatives (Chazdon, 2010).

Horizons provided the opportunity for the Center to be both community educators *and* coaches. The role of *Horizons* coaches evolved as communities worked through the four program components. Initially, they were directive to assure the communities understood program components. Later, coaches played more of a facilitative role as communities implemented their own collective vision for change. Meanwhile, Center educators provided support and links to helpful education and research. This collaboration of research-based programming and community coaching gave communities more control in studying and acting together.

Finally, Extension convened statewide resource organizations for a dialogue on the "state of rural communities in Minnesota." The dialogue encouraged participants' best thinking and generated ideas that people took back to their organizations. It generated partnerships the Center is still nurturing.

The Future

New initiatives are currently being developed for Horizons communities. One of these is the Voices of Rural Minnesota program. The Voices program, funded by NWAF, will build upon deliberative dialogue experiences in the Horizons program. The goal is to continue to bridge University resources with place-based, issue-specific engagement within Horizons communities.

The Voices program was developed because during the Horizons program, community members were frustrated that state and regional policies and programs were sometimes not relevant or accessible to rural communities. (For example, many grant programs require applicants to be a 501(c)3. Very small towns without nonprofit organizations are, for all practical purposes, not eligible for those grants.) Voices will create a speakers bureau that gives rural residents the opportunity to tell their stories and present their concerns to local, regional, and state policy makers and administrators. As multiple University departments and staff assist Voices participants with research and preparation, they will be introduced to or re-engaged with the values and principles of deliberative dialogue.

Conclusion

Horizons tested whether Land Grant Extension programs could deliver a place-based initiative that used public discourse as one tool that informed and motivated citizens to address poverty. *Horizons* proved successful on many fronts. The most impressive may be the extent to which *Horizons* increased university engagement. In Minnesota alone, 1,759 community members participated in poverty dialogues; 879 in leadership training; 5,391 in vision development. Over 47,000 volunteer hours were committed to implementing action strategies. Looking at all the states in the program, over 284 communities were engaged, over 2,400 facilitators trained, over 15,000 participated in dialogues, and over 6,600 participated in leadership training. Overall, 55,144 people participated in some component of the program.

The program also created local civic networks that grew in their capacity to work together and tackle problems. For example, many towns identified community gardens as an activity that could produce an immediate, tangible, and visible outcome. Once they successfully started community gardens, they turned their attention to teaching people how to prepare the food that was grown. This led to conversations about how they could increase the amount and variety of local healthy foods. Now, communities are talking about how they can generate physical activities that reduce obesity and diabetes—health conditions that are prevalent in communities with high poverty rates.

These civic networks also found the courage to leverage and grow available resources rather than rely on the positional authority of others to manage resources for them. "Buy local" campaigns became frequent *Horizons* projects, and in one town, the *Horizons* program provided small business start-up grants to residents aged eighteen to twenty-five. Minnesota's *Horizons* communities collectively report they have received $1,500,000 in new funding over the past five years for local projects. The total amount leveraged by community projects is still being counted as projects continue to develop and expand.

Horizons also had an effect on Extension. The program positioned Extension's community development programs—both within the university and among partnering organizations—as a vehicle to facilitate community change without prescribed answers and sparked new research.

Perhaps the definitive proof that *Horizons* has changed Extension is that the idea is being replicated. Recently, the Southern Rural Development Center launched the Turning the Tide on Poverty program (http://srdc .msstate.edu/tide). Using the *Thriving Communities* guide, the program will run in five states. They seek to "involve a wide range of community members in seeking a place based solution to poverty grounded in local talents and concerns and led by local voices."

The final note on *Horizons* as a formal program is yet to be written. In spring 2010, the NWAF decided to "pause" and assess the future of the program. Whatever the future, Extension will stay involved—with communities, with poverty, and in local conversations that matter. Dialogue is helping Extension realize Theodore Roosevelt's vision of a land grant system that creates "an effective community spirit," sustained by local energy, resources, and commitment.

References

Commission on County Life, "Report of the County Life Commission." 60th Congress, 2nd session, Document No. 705, 1909. Retrieved January 7, 2011 at http://ia700401.us .archive.org/12/items/cu31924085712861/cu31924085712861.pdf.
Chazdon, Scott and Stephanie Lott, Readiness for Engagement: A Qualitative Investigation of Community Social Capacity, University of Minnesota Extension, 2008.
Gladwell, M. *The Tipping Point.* New York: Little, Brown & Co., 2000.
Morse, G. W. *Cooperative Extension's Money and Mission Crisis: The Minnesota Response.* Bloomington, Ind.: Universe, 2009.
Peters, S. J. "Rousing the People on the Land: The Roots of the Educational Organizing Tradition in Extension Work." *Journal of Extension,* 2002, 40(3).
Pew Partnership for Civic Change. 2007. LeadershipPlenty®, Pew Partnerships for Civic Change. Retrieved from www.pew-partnership.org/lpinstitute.html.

MONICA HERRERA and JOYCE HOELTING *are staff of the University of Minnesota's Extension Center for Community Vitality. Monica is the Horizons program director. Joyce is the Center's assistant director.*

Campus-based centers and institutes serve as hubs for local dialogue, deliberation, and collaborative problem solving.

Facilitating Democracy: Centers and Institutes of Public Deliberation and Collaborative Problem Solving

Martín Carcasson

Facing significant budget deficits and stagnant enrollments, a local school district realized that they would likely need to close some schools, which is always a difficult issue for communities to consider. Initial newspaper reports about potential closings caused a strong reaction from the public, resulting in the organizing of several Facebook "Save our School" groups, angry letters to the editor of the local paper, and intense public meetings often vilifying the superintendent. The school district, hoping to find a way to have a productive community conversation about this difficult issue, turned to a local, nonpartisan university-based organization to help examine the situation from an impartial, third-party perspective, and then design, facilitate, and report on a public participation process. The organization utilized students throughout the process, including as facilitators of small group discussions during each of three large public meetings. In the end, the public engaged a difficult issue much more productively, the school district gained high-quality public input, students had an opportunity to gain valuable experience and sharpen their twenty-first century skills in a "real-world" situation, faculty researchers learned useful lessons about collaborative problem solving and deliberative practice, and the university bolstered its value to the community.

Projects such as these are happening more and more across the country in recent years. The continued development and maturation of campus-based centers and institutes tied to deliberative democracy, such as those that are a part of the National Issues Forum network and the University Network for Collaborative Governance (UNCG), represents a phenomenon that holds great promise to provide our communities with the necessary

New Directions for Higher Education, no. 152, Winter 2010 © Wiley Periodicals, Inc.
Published online in Wiley Online Library (wileyonlinelibrary.com) • DOI: 10.1002/he.412

capacity to spark and sustain productive collaborative problem solving. Such centers can serve as critical "hubs" of democracy that provide the necessary impartial resources and process expertise to connect experts, institutional decision makers, and the public in ways that democracy currently sorely lacks, but clearly requires to function well (Carcasson, 2008; London 2010). This chapter provides an introduction to these centers, an overview of the two networks, and a summary of the type of work they do.

Center Basics

The particular setup of the various centers varies widely. True to the nature of deliberative democracy, they are interdisciplinary, finding homes all over their respective colleges and universities. Many centers are stand-alone interdisciplinary entities of their own; others are connected to *academic disciplines* (currently there are centers housed in departments or schools of education, communication, government, law, business, history, political science, public health, urban planning, leadership, and community development), *administrative offices* (such as Offices of Equity and Diversity or Community Development), or *cooperative extension*. One of the UNCG centers, the Ruckelshaus Center, is a unique collaboration across two rival institutions, connecting the University of Washington and Washington State University.

The centers also differ significantly in size and budgets, in what activities they primarily focus upon, and the extent to which they utilize students or engage in research. Some of the centers are run by dedicated staff or tenured faculty, but more often the work of these centers is completed by individuals in a wide variety of positions whose work at the center makes up only a portion of their job descriptions. Despite these differences, two common threads bring these centers together. The first is an overall philosophy that has them focus on serving as key resources for improving the quality of collaborative decision making, problem solving, and public conflict management in their communities or regions. In other words, they focus on supporting processes designed to improve our democracy. To serve this mission, they cultivate a reputation of nonpartisan impartiality to play the critical roles of designers, conveners, facilitators, and reporters of productive collaborative processes such as community dialogues, deliberative forums, stakeholder negotiation processes, and other public participation efforts. Such processes require safe places for citizens to come together, good and fair information to help structure the conversation, and skilled facilitators to guide the process. In a variety of ways, these centers and institutes are dedicated to providing these three key ingredients to their respective communities.

Said differently, these centers often have a dual focus of addressing both the problems *in* democracy and the problems *of* democracy (Mathews, 2009). They help their communities address concrete public problems, but

Figure 6.1. Spheres of Democratic Communication.

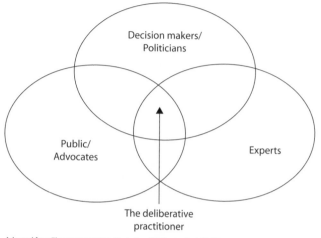

Adapted from Throgmorton, "The Rhetorics of Policy Analysis," 1991.

they hope to tackle them in particular ways that are more inclusive, lead to more sustainable solutions, and are supported more broadly by the community. In many ways, they also are concerned about building capacity and developing particular democratic habits in the community so that with each project the community becomes more self-sufficient (Carcasson, 2009).

A second common theme is that these centers generally support emerging notions of "democratic" or "collaborative" governance (Boyte, 2005; National League of Cities, 2006). Such perspectives call for a reconsideration of the respective roles of the public, experts, and government in public problem solving. They support the assumption that communities solve problems, not governments, though governments certainly remain a key tool for communities to utilize. Citizens are thus transformed from mere spectators, taxpayers, or voters, to engaged problem solvers. Such a view requires productive coordination between public, private, and nonprofit sectors; therefore, it necessitates processes that can support such interactions. As Figure 6.1 shows, deliberative practitioners such as those involved with these centers and institutes see themselves at the nexus of these worlds; they hope to facilitate bringing them together in much more productive ways to enable the coordination and refinement of interests and perspectives that democracy requires.

A Tale of Two Networks

Currently, two networks of such centers are operating and share many similarities, but also have some interesting differences. The National Issues

Forum (NIF) network has been developing for the last thirty years. Currently, fifty-two centers or institutes are listed on the NIF Web site, covering thirty-nine states (www.nifi.org/network). The network initially developed with a focus on training individuals to run public forums that would utilize NIF discussion guides. These centers hosted training workshops that primarily served to train community members how to host and moderate NIF-style public forums. The NIF forums typically involve two-hour sessions focused on a particular issue that brings the public together to consider a common problem and three or four potential approaches to addressing the problem. Such forums are often educational, but, at times, the data captured during the discussions may be used to spark community action, inform institutional decision makers, or contribute to broader research concerning the public voice on particular issues.These forums and workshops remain a key function of many of the NIF centers. Some of the centers focus on such NIF work, but most have a much wider range of activities. In particular, many of the most-involved centers have begun to focus more and more on engaging local issues, and thus develop original material for projects and experiment with a number of deliberative methods.

The University Network for Collaborative Governance (UNCG) is a newer network, but includes a number of centers with significant histories. In 2004, the Policy Consensus Initiative (PCI) conducted a national survey of around fifty university-based programs that were "providing consultation, convening, facilitation, training, research, and process-design services for collaborative policymaking efforts," and published the results in an insightful report entitled, "Finding Better Ways to Solve Public Problems: The Emerging Role of Universities as Neutral Forums for Collaborative Problem-Solving" (PCI, 2005). The report detailed the development and growth of many centers, lessons learned, and overviews of the activities with which they were involved. Following the report, PCI was instrumental in the development of UNCG, launched in 2008, and continues to play a key role in supporting the network. Quoting from the UNCG brochure, the network is "made up of forward-thinking centers and programs that engage in service and scholarship to enable citizens and their leaders to engage in dialogue, discussion, problem solving, and conflict resolution around public issues." Currently, twenty-six programs are officially part of the network.

Whereas the NIF network originated primarily to provide places for training, many UNCG centers began as centers focused on mediation, alternative dispute resolution, and collaborative policymaking, at times directly serving government agencies. Another distinction between the two networks is that a majority of the UNCG centers are focused on particular substantive issues such as natural resource management or intergovernmental relations, whereas the NIF centers tend to address a broader range of issues. It could perhaps also be said that the NIF centers typically focus more on working primarily with the general public and community organizations, whereas many of the UNCG programs are more involved with official stake-holder processes that are more likely to directly engage institutional decision makers and key organizational representatives rather than the general public. Stakeholder processes are also typically much more formal, involving multiple meetings, and at times seeking official consensus agreements. There are a few centers that are part of both networks, including the center that I direct at Colorado State University, the Center for Public Deliberation (CPD).

Center Activities

The centers and institutes in both networks participate in a wide range of activities. The two most basic activities are projects and training. In this sense, their work fits primarily, and for some centers exclusively, into service or engagement efforts in the collegiate triumvirate of teaching, research, and service. Projects may be a function of their university service, tied to class projects or student engagement, serve as a collaboration between the center and other campus or community organizations or government institutions, or be completed as part of a grant or fee-for-service contracts. Some of the more established UNCG centers are connected to state governments and work on major collaborative projects involving significant contracts. The centers may also provide specific services, particularly as process consultants and trained facilitators, for projects run by other organizations.

Most of the centers are also involved in training for a wide variety of skills connected to deliberative work, such as facilitation, issue framing, policy analysis, conflict management, and project design. Similar to the project work, the training at times is provided as a public service, and at times is a key revenue generator. Trainings may target the general public, community leaders, or local and state government officials. One of the current projects the UNCG is taking on is to perform an inventory of both the collaborative competencies related to the work and the various trainings offered among the centers in order to create better coordination between them.

Beyond these two major activities that are common to many of the centers, other activities depend on the particular program. The degree to which centers are connected to teaching and research varies significantly. A growing number of the NIF centers in particular utilize students in many aspects of their programs. Projects run by the CPD at Colorado State University, for example, involve students throughout. A student associate program was developed that brings in about ten to fifteen students each semester through an application process to participate in a year-long program. During the first semester, students take a dedicated three-hour course focused on training them as facilitators, and then in subsequent semesters take practicum credits while working on projects. Students assist in all aspects of CPD projects, including project selection, design, convening, facilitating, and reporting. Such substantial student involvement is not typical of many of the programs,

NEW DIRECTIONS FOR HIGHER EDUCATION • DOI: 10.1002/he

however. Other programs may have internships for students, or have specific programs to attract students to training workshops, but do not rely heavily on the students during projects.

Lastly, some of the centers are also involved in research, particularly on public policy issues. Many of the NIF centers work closely with the Kettering Foundation, a research foundation that focuses on the question, "What does it take to make democracy work as it should?" Research, however, is typically a secondary concern. Research may be focused on deliberative theory and practice, or on the specific issues their projects address. Many develop detailed case studies of their projects, though the degree to which such work is considered "research" likely depends on the institution.

Conclusion: Future Growth and Development

Centers can serve as clearinghouses and symbolic institutional homes for the variety of critical activities that require significant capacity and time to do well. Activities such as being the local voice for civility and collaboration, linking and improving theory and practice, serving as a central organizing point for grant proposals and fee-for-service work, providing training opportunities and faculty development, and connecting the work to students and faculty in multiple disciplines. The future development of these centers, however, will be contingent on a number of factors. Much of the work of these centers is completed by individual deliberative catalysts or entrepreneurs that often go significantly "above and beyond" in time and effort to support the work of their organizations. Such a model is not sustainable long term. Many of the centers are also in precarious financial positions at their institutions, as are any university entities that are not directly connected to core functions. The ability of these centers to acquire more resources, particularly in the form of dedicated staff, is critical to the impact they have on our communities. Some of the centers are self-sufficient through fee-for-service, but if forced to rely on charging for their services, their impact on their communities may be limited to projects that have financial support, which can lead to inequalities. Perhaps most important to their future development and sustainability is having them more strongly connect to the teaching and research functions of their institutions, without distracting from the important service work they currently provide. In the end, perhaps the ultimate vision is for every college or university across the country to provide all their students with the skills our diverse democracy requires, take responsibility in their research efforts to better understand *and* improve the quality of our democratic processes, and serve their communities as catalysts, conveners, and facilitators for deliberative practice. As stories similar to the one that opened this essay are replicated more and more across the country, it seems clear that centers and institutes specifically focused on deliberative democracy and collaborative problem solving offer a particularly promising way to fulfill those responsibilities.

References

Boyte, H. C. "Reframing Democracy: Governance, Civic Agency, and Politics." *Public Administration Review,* 2005, *65*(5), 536–546.

Carcasson, M. "Beginning with the End in Mind: A Call for Goal Driven Deliberation." Center for the Advancement of Public Engagement Occasional Paper #2, 2009. Retrieved April 4, 2010, from http://www.publicagenda.com/cape.

Carcasson, M. "Democracy's Hubs: College and University Centers as Platforms for Deliberative Practice." Kettering Foundation Research Report. Dayton, OH: Kettering Foundation, 2008.

London, S. *Doing Democracy: How a Network of Grassroots Organizations Is Strengthening Community, Building Capacity, and Shaping a New Kind of Civic Education.* Dayton, Ohio: A Report for the Kettering Foundation, 2010. Retrieved January 7, 2011, from http://www.kettering.org/media_room/publications/Doing-Democracy.

Mathews, D. "Afterwards: Ships Passing in the Night?" In D. Barker and D. Brown (eds.), *A Different Kind of Politics: Readings on the Role of Higher Education in Democracy.* Dayton, OH: Kettering Foundation Press, 2009.

National League of Cities. *Strengthening Democratic Governance. Changing the Way We Govern: Building Democratic Governance in Your Community.* Washington, D.C.: National League of Cities, 2006.

Policy Consensus Initiative. *Finding Better Ways to Solve Public Problems: The Emerging Role of Universities as Neutral Forums for Collaborative Policymaking.* 2005. Retrieved April 4, 2010, from http://www.policyconsensus.org/publications/reports/docs/UniversityReport.pdf.

Throgmorton, J. A. "The Rhetorics of Policy Analysis." *Policy Sciences,* 1991, *24,* 153–179.

MARTIN CARCASSON is an associate professor in Communication Studies at Colorado State University.

7

Action research is a promising vehicle for filling gaps in our knowledge of deliberation and democratic governance.

Research for Democracy and Democracy for Research

Kiran Cunningham, Matt Leighninger

Attempts to involve citizens more productively in public life have proliferated so rapidly that scholars are struggling to catch up. Around the world, community leaders are experimenting with ways to engage residents in public deliberation, decision making, and problem solving. A number of questions and challenges facing public officials, civic practitioners, community organizers, and other leaders could benefit from closer attention by academic researchers. Moreover, aside from these gaps in our collective knowledge, the democratic principles evident in the new wave of public engagement initiatives present another challenge to the academy: how to involve citizens more effectively in the research process itself?

The complex, continually shifting landscape of citizenship and democracy presents ample challenges for the researcher. When it comes to measuring the outcomes of engagement efforts, there are three principal complications:

- Deliberative democracy can generate outcomes at different levels, from individual attitudes and behavior to small-group actions to organizational shifts to policy changes, so trying to understand the outcomes of any given project requires quite a broad scope of inquiry.
- The leaders and organizers who initiate these attempts to engage citizens have diverse and numerous goals, which are often not clearly articulated beforehand.
- The outcomes of an initiative are also dependent on the goals and concerns that the participants (citizens) bring to the table—and the goals of the "involvers" may or may not match the goals of the "involved."

New Directions for Higher Education, no. 152, Winter 2010 © Wiley Periodicals, Inc.
Published online in Wiley Online Library (wileyonlinelibrary.com) • DOI: 10.1002/he.413

These democratic complications defy traditional models of research and evaluation, and mesh well with the principles of engaged scholarship and action research. We are faced, then, with a two-sided question: how might researchers contribute to the development of democracy—and how might democratic principles contribute to that research?

In suggesting some answers to this question, we will attempt to summarize the existing research on the impacts of deliberative democracy, as well as the gaps where more research is needed. Then, we will use several examples to illustrate how action research can be a particularly effective methodology for democracy scholarship and evaluation.

Public Engagement and Deliberative Democracy

Much of the existing research on public engagement and deliberative democracy has clustered on how people communicate in deliberative settings, and how these experiences affect their attitudes and behavior. A number of key group process techniques have emerged in this field, such as impartial facilitation, ground rules set by the group, and a discussion guide that lays out a range of views or options. We are learning from a number of studies (Polletta, 2008; Muhlberger, 2006; Black, 2008; Ryfe, 2006) that when these tactics are used, the way participants interact is generally positive in the sense that it conforms to the kinds of conversations people want: respectful, thoughtful, enlightening, balanced, and inspiring. These deliberative experiences are, however, different in some important respects from what many of the theorists anticipated: the discussions typically feature storytelling, passion, humor, and conflict (Walsh, 2007; Mansbridge, Hartz-Karp, Amengual, and Gastil, 2006; Black, 2008; Ryfe, 2006). In other words, deliberative democracy in practice is far more emotional, cathartic, and complex than the purely rational, reasoned stereotypes prevalent in theories of deliberative democracy.

We are also learning, from program evaluations as well as in-depth academic studies (Muhlberger, 2006; Abelson and Gauvin, 2006), that this work usually affects individuals; generally speaking, they become more informed, modify their policy opinions, gain a greater appreciation of the views and values of others, and gain higher levels of trust in government, in other institutions, and in other citizens generally.

We have compiled many stories and case studies—almost entirely qualitative—of projects that have achieved some larger impact on public policy (Fung and Fagotto, 2009; Leighninger, 2006; Friedman and Kadlec, 2007a; Levine and Torres, 2008; see also the growing resource, Participedia.net). In some cases, the most notable outcomes occurred at a different level than the organizers expected (i.e., small-group actions instead of policy change, or policy change instead of changes in individual behavior). Will Friedman, Alison Kadlec, and others have moved beyond the visionary, almost Platonic tone that has flavored many academic works on deliberation and begun to

NEW DIRECTIONS FOR HIGHER EDUCATION • DOI: 10.1002/he

explore the *realpolitik* of how power influences, and is influenced by, deliberative democracy (Friedman and Kadlec, 2007b).

Gaps in the Current Research

One of the most common general critiques of the literature on deliberative democracy, along with many other approaches to social change, is that there are very few quantitative studies. Impacts on individuals are easier to quantify because they tend to rely on pre- and post-surveys, but few researchers have attempted to quantify effects on public policy making or problem solving.

There are a number of more specific areas where further research might illuminate the lessons and challenges of deliberative democracy on the ground:

- *Variables for Measuring Policy Impact.* What are the variables that can help us understand the relationship between deliberative democracy initiatives and the likelihood of policy change? Miriam Wyman and Vera Schattan Coehlo suggest inclusion, connections, and legitimacy as three critical and potentially measurable factors (Wyman and Coehlo, 2010). Can these or other factors help practitioners decide how to connect citizen voices with policy-making processes?
- *Variables for Assessing "Embeddedness."* Similarly, are there factors or variables that can help measure "embeddedness"—the extent to which democratic principles have been incorporated into the regular patterns and processes of local governance? Most attempts to engage citizens are temporary efforts focused on a specific issue or policy decision; even when they are successful, the democratic strategies and principles they employ are seldom incorporated into the way communities function. From their study of several communities that seem to have embedded public deliberation, Archon Fung and Elena Fagotto propose political authority, deliberative capacity, and demand for democracy as conditions for embeddedness (Fung and Fagotto, 2009).
- *Connections Between Engagement and Economic Growth.* The twenty-six-city "Soul of the Community," conducted by the Gallup Corporation (Washington, D.C.) and supported by the Ford Foundation (New York), argues that there is a positive correlation between the citizens' sense of attachment to community and the rate of economic growth in that city (www.soulofthecommunity.org). Does this finding hold up in other studies? Does public engagement have a measurable impact on residents' sense of attachment, and how might local leaders and practitioners modify their tactics in order to maximize that impact?
- *Connections Between Online and Face-to-Face Deliberation.* More and more public engagement work is taking place online. Leaders and organizers use a range of online tools and formats for recruitment, issue framing, action planning, and in some cases, actual dialogue and deliberation.

NEW DIRECTIONS FOR HIGHER EDUCATION • DOI: 10.1002/he

Some studies have explored the quality and characteristics of moderated online communication (Stromer-Galley, 2008; Muhlberger, 2006), but there has been little research that explores how online and face-to-face communication can best complement one another.

- *Exploring Cost-Benefit Analysis.* Is it possible to frame decisions about whether and when to engage the public in a form that public managers readily understand: the cost-benefit analysis? Intensive public engagement is usually characterized as time- and resource-intensive, but those expenditures are often hard to determine—and the time and resources required for traditional, nonparticipatory decision-making processes are seldom factored into the comparison. (The British nonprofit organization, Involve, is taking up this question in a new study.)
- *Connections Between "Representative Sample" and "Critical Mass" Approaches.* One of the main strategic differences in this work is between initiatives that aim to construct a demographically representative "random sample" of the population, and those that aim to assemble a diverse "critical mass" of participants. These methodologies have typically been conducted in isolation from one another, even though they seem anecdotally to have different strengths and weaknesses, and may have more potential when combined as distinct activities in an overarching democracy strategy. Researchers could guide experimentation along these lines by testing these strengths and weaknesses and examining the few cases where both strategies are evident.

This is only a small sample of possible directions for future research. As observers and supporters of democratic innovation, they seem important to us—and yet we feel that the interests and knowledge needs of ordinary citizens who are at the center of democratic innovation are even more important. The people who participate in these new democratic arenas need to be able to shape the goals of processes, measure their progress and outcomes, and modify their strategies to achieve greater success. Incorporating an action research methodology into the research and evaluation process has the potential to bring the practices of deliberative democracy and the procedures by which they are assessed into philosophical alignment.

Action Research as a Tool for Democratizing Research

Action research is a social change-oriented form of research rooted in collaborative inquiry (see Cunningham and McKinney, 2010, for a more thorough discussion of how action research fits into the broader category of engaged scholarship). According to Greenwood and Levin, action research "generates knowledge claims for the express purpose of taking action to promote social change and social analysis. . . .[It] aims to increase the ability of the involved community or organization members to control their own destinies more effectively and to keep improving their capacity to do so" (Greenwood and Levin, 1998, p. 6). It begins with real-life problems, an understanding of which is arrived at through deliberative processes that then lead to new meanings out of which stem social action. Recent recipients of the New England Research Center for Higher Education's Lynton Award are excellent examples of scholars engaging in action research. Michelle Dunlap's work with underserved, minority communities in southeastern Connecticut; Lorlene Hoyt's work with the City of Lawrence and its various constituent groups in the areas of affordable housing, asset building, and sustainability; and Nick Tobier's work in Detroit with publicly oriented art, all engage teams of students and community members in problem identification, collaborative research, and problem solving (New England Research Center for Higher Education, 2010).

At Kalamazoo College (Kalamazoo, Michigan), we used an action research methodology to build democracy into the design of a deliberative dialogues initiative. As communities of people living and working together, campuses are microcosms of democratic societies. Like many communities, their functioning depends on hierarchical structures of various sorts and people with unequal status. Moreover, campus communities tend to be very concerned with creating "community," the discourse around which often involves masking, both intentionally and unintentionally, the injustices associated with these hierarchical structures. Given these characteristics, campuses are ripe for both the practice and study of deliberative democracy.

The deliberative dialogues initiative at Kalamazoo College was a key component of the launching of the College's new Arcus Center for Social Justice Leadership. The process centered around two framing questions, "What is social justice?" and "What does a socially just campus look like?" The goals of the dialogues included developing a shared understanding of the term "social justice," generating a shared vision of Kalamazoo College as a socially just community, developing a plan for achieving that vision, and modeling exemplary practices of public dialogue and deliberation. In addition, the process was designed to generate useful baseline assessment data for the Arcus Center about how social (in)justice is understood and experienced on campus. The participants included hourly staff, facilities management staff, administrative staff, faculty, and students.

Designed in consultation with Everyday Democracy, the dialogues were implemented through a class called Dialogues for Social Justice. The members of the class included twelve students, three staff members, and two faculty members. The course itself was designed both as an action research project and as the vehicle through which the dialogues would be facilitated, conducted, and analyzed. Core texts included Ernest Stringer's *Action Research* (2007) and Iris Marion Young's *Inclusion and Democracy* (2000). Everyday Democracy trained thirty-two facilitators, which included the sixteen class members and a second set of sixteen faculty, staff, and students who served as co-facilitators for the study circles. Subsequently, we held six-teen concurrent sets of three study circles and an additional abbreviated study circle process for people on campus who were not able to commit to the three-session study circle process. In addition, we held an open poster session to engage the community in a discussion of the findings from the dialogues and an action forum to engage the campus community in the process of identifying the college's strongest assets, biggest challenges, and the highest priority actions the college should engage in to become a socially just campus. Out of a total campus population of roughly 2,000 people, 303 staff, faculty, and students participated in the process.

Consistent with action research principles, the community was involved in the project all along the way. Class members, who included stu-dents, support staff, faculty and administrative staff, were involved in the project design, recorded field notes from the study circles, analyzed the data, interpreted the data through theoretical lenses, and wrote up the results. In addition, through the poster session and the action forum, members of the campus community collaborated in analyzing the findings, identifying key challenges and assets, and prioritizing action steps.

As a result, members of various constituent groups on campus were able to enhance their capacity to generate knowledge and to be more effec-tive participants in democracy. Using Greenwood and Levin's terms, the proj-ect enhanced the ability of community members to "control their own destinies more effectively and to keep improving their capacity to do so" (Greenwood and Levin, 1998, p. 6). Indeed, one could argue that social jus-tice was furthered and the capacity of the institution to become a commu-nity grounded in a commitment to social justice was increased.

The Kalamazoo College process offers useful insight into the kinds of questions researchers should consider as we work toward developing a methodological framework for democratizing research on democracy. For example:

• How can we design all stages of the research and evaluation process to engage the community with whom the dialogues will be conducted as co-researchers—including designing the research, gathering the data, ana-lyzing the data, generating reports, designing the evaluation plan, and implementing the changes that the evaluation process calls for?
• How can every stage of the process be an opportunity for the co-generation of new knowledge about the problem itself?
• How can every stage of the research be, itself, truly inclusive and delib-erative?

These kinds of questions are similar to those asked by action researchers and also by Guba and Lincoln (1989) in their book, *Fourth Gen-eration Evaluation*. The research called for here, however, takes that work a step further by incorporating the principles of deep inclusion, the practices of deliberation, and a commitment to the co-generation of knowledge, not by researchers and participants or key stakeholders, but by co-researchers engaged in a research process grounded in deliberative processes of democratic knowledge generation for social change.

Citizens as Researchers

If the growth of deliberative democracy is a reaction to the changing capacities and expectations of citizens, then the ways in which this work is researched and evaluated should also reflect that new reality in democratic governance. Indeed, at some point citizens may demand this sort of shift and begin to question evaluations that are not responsive to the needs and goals of participants. However, this is a negative way of viewing the challenge: even if citizen voices remain absent from the research debate, evaluators should consider the positive potential of ordinary people to contribute to documentation, evaluation, and assessment. Just as deliberative democracy initiatives aim to increase community capacity by mobilizing citizens as problem solvers, research on deliberative democracy can increase knowledge-building by mobilizing citizens as researchers.

To pursue this larger potential of research for democracy and democracy for research, practitioners, researchers, and others—including interested citizens—we will need to take on some of the questions listed in this chapter. We need a greater shared understanding of what we want to learn and how we might learn it, and we need to develop and disseminate tools for gathering that knowledge. If we can accomplish these tasks, we will not only be learning more about deliberative democracy, we will be enhancing the capacity of all of us to bring about the kind of society we seek.

References

Abelson, J., and Gauvin, F. *Assessing the Impacts of Public Participation: Concepts, Evidence, and Policy Implications*. Ottawa, Ontario: Canadian Policy Research Networks, 2006.

Black, L. "Deliberation, Storytelling, and Dialogic Moments." *Communication Theory*, 2008, *18*, 93–116.

Cunningham, K., and McKinney, H. "Towards the Recognition and Integration of Action Research and Deliberative Democracy." *Journal of Public Deliberation*, 2010. Retrieved June 15, 2010, from http://services.bepress.com/jpd/vol6/iss1/.

Friedman, W., and Kadlec, A. *A Decade of Public Engagement in Bridgeport*. New York: Public Agenda, 2007a.

Friedman, W., and Kadlec, A. "Deliberative Democracy and Problem of Power." *Journal of Public Deliberation*, 2007b, *3*, Article 8. Retrieved June 15, 2010, from http://services .bepress .com/jpd/vol2/iss3/art8/.

Fung, A., and Fagotto, E. *Sustaining Public Engagement: Embedded Deliberation*. Dayton, Ohio: Everyday Democracy and Kettering Foundation, 2009.

Greenwood, D., and Levin, M. *Introduction to Action Research: Social Research for Social Change*. Thousand Oaks, Calif.: Sage Publications, 1998.

Guba, E., and Lincoln, Y. *Fourth Generation Evaluation*. Thousand Oaks, Calif.: Sage, 1989.

Leighninger, M. *The Next Form of Democracy: How Expert Rule Is Giving Way to Shared Governance—And Why Politics Will Never Be the Same*. Nashville, Tenn.: Vanderbilt University Press, 2006.

Levine, P., and Torres, L. *Where Is Democracy Headed? Research and Practice on Public Deliberation*. Washington, D.C.: Deliberative Democracy Consortium, 2008.

Mansbridge, J., Hartz-Karp, J., Amengual, M., and Gastil, J. "Norms of Deliberation: An Inductive Study." *Journal of Public Deliberation*, 2006, 2, Article 7. Retrieved June 7, 2010, from http://services.bepress.com/jpd/vol2/iss1/art7/.

Muhlberger, P. "Report to the Deliberative Democracy Consortium: Building a Deliberation Measurement Toolbox, 2006." Retrieved March 15, 2010, from http://www.geocities.com/pmuhl78/abstracts.html#VirtualAgoraReport.

New England Research Center for Higher Education. "Past Lynton Award Recipients, 2010." Retrieved June 17, 2010, from http://www.nerche.org/index.php?option=com_content&view=article&id=74&catid=25&Itemid=55.

Polletta, F. "Just Talk: Public Deliberation after 9/11." *Journal of Public Deliberation*, 2008, 4, Article 2. Retrieved June 14, 2010, from http://services.bepress.com/jpd/vol4/iss1/art2.

Ryfe, D. "Narrative and Deliberation in Small Group Forums." *Journal of Applied Communication Research*, 2006, 34, 72–93.

Stringer, E. *Action Research* (3rd ed.). Thousand Oaks, Calif.: Sage, 2007.

Stromer-Galley, J. "Measuring Deliberation's Content: A Coding Scheme." *Journal of Public Deliberation*, 2008, 3, Article 12. Retrieved June 15, 2010, from http://services.bepress.com/jpd/vol3/iss1/art12/.

Walsh, K. *Talking about Race: Community Dialogues and the Politics of Disagreement*. Chicago: University of Chicago Press, 2007.

Wyman, M., Barrett, G., and Coehlo, V. "Policy Impacts of Deliberative Public Engagement." In T. Nabatchi, M. Weiksner, J. Gastil, and M. Leighninger (eds.), *Democracy in Motion: Evaluating the Practice and Impact of Deliberative Civic Engagement*. Submitted for publication.

Young, I. *Inclusion and Democracy*. Oxford: Oxford University Press, 2000.

KIRAN CUNNINGHAM *is a professor of Anthropology at Kalamazoo College.*

MATT LEIGHNINGER *is executive director of the Deliberative Democracy Consortium.*

8

The dynamics of institutional power need to be addressed through structural practices that support prospects for authentic, democratic partnerships.

Power, Privilege, and the Public: The Dynamics of Community-University Collaboration

Byron P. White

Scholars, practitioners, and proponents of community–university engagement insist that reciprocity, mutual benefit, and peer relationships are essential to creating truly democratic partnerships between campus and community leaders (Bringle and Hatcher, 2002; Peters, 2005; Weerts and Sandmann, 2008). These same principles are seen as important to creating environments where university students learn democratic knowledge, skills, and values through civic engagement (Boyte and Kari, 2002; Creighton, 2009; Hartley and Hollander, 2005). Frequently, the effort to carry out these principles focuses on the quality of interpersonal relations. It is aimed at the way individuals—students, faculty, and administrators—interact with community representatives, particularly where cultural, economic, and educational differences are apparent.

   Achieving democratic partnerships must also take into account discrepancies in power and privilege between the conditions of the university as an institution and the conditions of the community as a whole. Unfortunately, this macro-level relationship is seldom discussed in the literature on community-university engagement. It is as though campus participants believe—or hope—that positive personal relationships between university and citizen actors can somehow surmount the overriding social disparities between campus and community.

   My research and experience suggest that although constructive interpersonal relationships may mitigate and even postpone inevitable conflicts between institution and community, they cannot eliminate them. No matter how personally well-liked a university representative may be to the community or how prominent the rhetoric of community–university parity exists in

New Directions for Higher Education, no. 152, Winter 2010 © Wiley Periodicals, Inc.
Published online in Wiley Online Library (wileyonlinelibrary.com) • DOI: 10.1002/he.414

the university's purpose statement, the university almost always is richer, has greater professional capacity, controls more resources, and is more politically connected than the community. Well-intentioned university representatives may elude this reality; it is never overlooked by the community.

If universities are to be places that foster democratic practices—both in student learning and institutional engagement—they will need to implement institutional strategies that address the unique challenges created by the disparity in power and privilege between campus and community.

Differences in Power and Privilege

The inequity between most colleges and universities and the communities that surround them can be rather dramatic. In most cases, the residents surrounding the university would not qualify to be enrolled as students. Often, they would not be qualified to hold most of the jobs there. At Ohio State University (OSU), located in the center of metropolitan Columbus, one need only drive a block east of High Street to realize immediately that the bordering neighborhood of Weinland Park, with its 5,000 residents, pales in stature to the university community, which has eight times as many employees. As one Ohio State administrator said, "You know, High Street, it might as well be the Mississippi River from that neighborhood to here, it is such a divider" (White, 2008, p. 2).

The average household income in Weinland Park was $15,381, according to a City of Columbus report published in 2006 (p. 52). A 2010 survey by Ohio State researchers found that only 18 percent of respondents held full-time jobs (Forrest and Goldstein, 2010, p. 6). The city report found that only 9 percent of the neighborhood's housing units were owned by neighborhood residents and much of the community's housing was in disrepair, a stark contrast to OSU's well-groomed 1,756-acre main campus. Although upscale stores like Urban Outfitters line High Street next to campus, a Dollar Tree bargain store is one of the most prominent businesses on the street as it runs through Weinland Park. More than 52,000 students are working on OSU degrees; however, only 31 percent of Weinland Park's residents had attended college and 38 percent did not even have a high school diploma, according to the city report.

Such dramatic differences are not only the case where campuses border inner-city communities, but also in quaint college towns that seem to reflect the same profile of the colleges and universities that abide there. The Web sites for Cornell University and Ithaca College both refer affectionately to the city of Ithaca, New York, where the institutions are located. One site calls the city "a blend of rural practicality, urban sophistication, and international flavor . . . that produces the warmth and friendliness of a small town combined with the rich cultural complexity of places many times larger" ("The Ithaca Campus," 2010). Yet, a 2010 report by the New York Community Action Agency, noted a more ominous aspect of life in Ithaca: It had the highest poverty rate—40.5 percent—of twenty-six cities the agency analyzed based on data from its county affiliates (*New York State Poverty Report*). Median income in Ithaca was $29,236, less than the tuition for Ithaca College ($33,630) and Cornell ($39,450), according to their Web sites.

The imbalance of privilege and power plays a powerful role in shaping the perceptions of community partners. For them, the implications of this disparity are obvious and simple. As the head of one civic association in Weinland Park told me about Ohio State, "They got the resources; they can do whatever they want to do" (White, 2008, p. 89).

The Community's Dualistic Perspective

I have found in my research of community engagement between Ohio State and Weinland Park, and through my experience working with Xavier University and the Cincinnati neighborhoods that border its campus, that this perception of the university's overwhelming abundance persists even when individuals at the institution demonstrate their intentions to engage the community more democratically.

Jen Gilbride-Brown, formerly the senior program director for faculty and campus development for Ohio Campus Compact, learned this lesson during her days as a graduate teaching assistant at OSU. As a doctoral student in what was then OSU's College of Education, Gilbride-Brown was teaching a course called Leadership for the Common Good, which included a community engagement component. Over two academic quarters, about thirty of her students worked at a nonprofit family resource center housed in the basement of a church in the nearby university district.

During the fall quarter, the resource center learned that it was losing the grant that funded the majority of the its $125,000 annual operating budget. The program director asked Gilbride-Brown if OSU would provide $10,000 to help cover the shortage. Gilbride-Brown recalls that she was shocked that the program director would ask her—a financially strapped graduate student with no access to a significant university budget—to find the money. It was then that she realized that to the organization's staff, regardless of their personal relationship with her, she represented mighty Ohio State University with its vast resources and $4.5 billion budget.

"Initially it was just laughable that she saw me as part of the university," Gilbride-Brown says, reflecting on the situation. "I'm just a first-year doc student. We had gotten to know each other personally. We were pals. But when I thought about it, I didn't think it was an unfair request for the institution."

Gilbride-Brown tried to drum up the money on campus to no avail. Within six months, the organization ceased operation. I have heard Gilbride-Brown share this story with faculty from other universities and they almost unanimously agree that the community's request was inappropriate and outside the scope of the relationship. Nevertheless, to leaders of community-based organizations, there is no such distinction. Their interactions with the university take place, simultaneously, on two levels: There is the interpersonal level, where relationships are forged with individual representatives from the university. Then there is the institutional level, where the university's abundance of power and privilege can be a resource or a threat (White, 2009). This dualistic engagement can lead to tensions and power struggles between campus and community.

Such tensions can be exacerbated by racial differences and the historical legacy of white oppression. In that sense, race plays a role in defining the power and privilege dynamic between predominantly white universities' minority communities. However, I have found that cultural differences or similarities concerning race to be secondary factors to the tangible evidence of discrepancy in resources and clout. As an African American university administrator with a deep affinity toward and familiarity with the black community, I certainly possessed some advantages in relationship-building over my white colleagues. However, I was not necessarily any more effective at assuaging the community's concerns about the university's power. Although cultural affinity may impact the community's interpersonal perspective, it is not sufficient to overcome the power imbalance the community calculates at the institutional level.

Navigating the Power Imbalance

If universities are to play a greater role at educating effective citizens and serving as catalysts for social, economic, and political transformation through authentic civic engagement, then they will have to learn to understand, anticipate, and navigate the community's two-tiered perspective. Doing so will require more than friendly overtures; it will take intentional administrative actions that are built on principles of deliberative democracy, where the university places as great an emphasis on fostering self-determination and self-rule among citizens as it does on demonstrating the impact of university programs. I propose three fundamental practices for accomplishing this: (1) be transparent, (2) send the right people, and (3) share authority.

Be Transparent. It is not always *what* we do in higher education that most concerns the community, but *why* we do what we do. Higher education officials spend so much time defending what they are doing for the community that they often fail to provide a convincing rationale for what is driving their intentions. We may offer an altruistic explanation—to improve the community and help our students learn—but we avoid the more selfish motives that also are involved, such as fulfilling a grant requirement, raising the institution's public reputation, improving our competitive advantage among other institutions, appeasing a donor's interests, or advancing our research agenda. Of course, the community knows that we expect something out of the deal; if higher education officials are not upfront in sharing what that is, the community will invent our intentions for us.

I learned this lesson a few years ago when Xavier University (Cincinnati, Ohio) purchased a historic building in the nearby Evanston neighborhood that was to have been abandoned. In renovating the building for university office space—including offices dedicated to community engagement—the university saw itself as contributing to the community's well-being. However, neighborhood leaders saw it as a sign that Xavier wanted to buy up property in their community. The fact that the university could acquire a major structure at its will using its own resources demonstrated a level of potentially threatening power that the community could not match.

The only way to move past these underlying suspicions is for colleges and universities to be more open and transparent about their affairs: their operations, their strategic goals, their decision-making processes. Consider how much detail the university has to know about the community before feeling confident enough to engage it. Demographic data, needs analyses, and meetings with community leaders are all part of the fundamental research necessary before entering into a community partnership. Yet community members usually do not have access to comparable information about the university. They typically have no idea about the university's budget, particularly the resources dedicated to the partnership. They do not know the agendas of the individuals who authorize the project. Many never even get to see the syllabus for the course the students are taking who show up in the community, let alone read an article published by the professor teaching the course to understand her research focus.

Certainly, committed partners in the community deserve to know what goes on behind higher education's veil if they are to trust the university as an institution, and not just select individuals. Although such disclosure carries a level of risk, those who have taken this route have found the community to be far more likely to guard the privilege of being an insider than to abuse it.

Karen Hutzel, an art education professor at OSU, instructs her community partners on the purpose and process of the university's institutional review board so that there is clear understanding in the community of the guidelines for her research related to their work together. In doing so, her partners have played a role in designing research procedures that meet both scholarly and community objectives. At Xavier, we established the Evanston–Norwood–Xavier Community Partnership—with eight members from each community—to serve as a kind of sounding board for sensitive university information that could affect the community. Through the exchange, community participants have contributed critical guidance to several of the university's strategic initiatives. Others have called for collaboratively written guidelines for community–university partnerships that allow community partners to negotiate the details of the partnership.

Choose the Right University Representatives. Harwood and Creighton (2009) suggest that leaders of civic-serving institutions, such as universities, though committed to principles of community engagement, are sometimes reluctant to practice it in part because of their misgivings about selecting the "right" partner who truly represents the community. However, institutions tend to be far less particular about who represents the university. Typically, the person managing the project becomes the representative by default. Beyond that, many would say that an ability to engage interpersonally across educational, economic, cultural, and racial barriers is important. However, given the community's dualistic view of the relationship with the university, having the right interpersonal skills is not enough. The best representative also would have a level of institutional authority to adequately respond to the expectations of the community. To have one capacity without the other can be problematic.

For instance, faculty members who engage community partners sometimes operate in a kind of "freelance mode," separating themselves from the bureaucracy of their institutions to operate more freely as part of the community. It feels good from a relational standpoint, but when they are called upon to satisfy the demands made on their home institutions, they are ill equipped to do so. In other cases, the university representative might be an administrator who has enough authority to address real concerns with institutional power, but who lacks the appropriate interpersonal skills—or may be reluctant to use them. They adopt a more "sheltered mode" of engagement, choosing not to extend themselves too intimately into the community and relying on more formal methods of interaction (White, 2009).

The ideal candidate to represent the university in a partnership, then, would operate in a "balanced mode," possessing both these qualities: sensitivity to community and a sufficient level of authority. Such roles do not typically exist in higher education. They usually have to be created intentionally with strategic foresight on the part of the university. Even if such an ideal person is not available, institutions can be deliberate about linking the interpersonal capacity to institutional authority by making sure faculty and others on the front lines are working collaboratively with an administrative structure on campus, whether an academic department or an office devoted to community engagement.

Share Authority. At a three-day summit hosted in 2006 by Community-Campus Partnerships for Health (CCHP), experienced community partners from across the country agreed that authentic community-university partnerships require there to be "shared resources, power and decision-making" (CCHP, 2007, p. 7). They also acknowledged that this rarely happens. Universities and colleges may ask community residents what their needs and aspirations are in the partnership. They establish advisory boards to allow for a "community voice." They set up interviews and focus groups with community leaders to gain their input.

Nevertheless, advice and input are not the same as authority. More often than not, such overtures amount to gathering insider information so that the real people in power can use it to make final decisions. Shared authority exists when a partner has the certainty—not the hope—that its desires will impact the actions of the other partner. There is a litmus test for telling who holds it in greater abundance: the party that decides how money is spent and how individuals' time is deployed. As the CCHP summit report bluntly noted, "Whoever holds the purse strings, holds the power" (CCHP, p. 11).

More often than not, such power falls into the hands of the college or university. The grant that funds the project typically is given to the institution of higher education. The personnel deployed to work on the project—staff or students—are usually under some direct supervision of a university employee. It seems perfectly rational that this would be the case given the university's ordinarily superior fiscal record of accomplishment and staff capacity. However, the "fiscal agent" defense does little to reconcile the community's sense of being dominated.

I was once confronted by a group of community leaders who questioned the way my university was spending grant money that was dedicated to a community partnership. They argued that the performance of a nonprofit organization, with which I had contracted as part of the grant, was underperforming and that another community-based group, which the leaders favored, would do a better job. In that moment, as the one who authorized the checks, I held all the power in the so-called partnership. It took a tense conversation and some soul-searching on my part to concede that the community leaders were right and to allow them to oversee that aspect of the budget. If we are serious about bridging the gap of power and privilege, then community partners must have some means to exercise direct authority in dictating the allocation of resources involved in the partnership as a fundamental part of the decision-making structure.

Conclusion

Institutions of higher education can never really even the playing field with the communities with which we engage. Even the best interpersonal relations between university and community representatives cannot overcome the power and privilege that favor higher education. However, by engaging communities more as peers at the institutional level, colleges and universities can come closer to approximating democratic partnership that has the potential to lead to sustainable transformation of both the community and the academy. Moreover, by operating in this manner, universities set an example for their students to follow and create a constructive platform for them to work from as they are formed into citizens who are equipped to make a difference in the civic life of their communities.

References

Boyte, H. C., and Kari, N. N. "Renewing the Democratic Spirit in American Colleges and Universities: Higher Education as Public Work." In T. Ehrlich (ed.), *Civic Responsibility and Higher Education*. Phoenix: Oryx Press, 2002.

Bringle, R. G., and Hatcher, J. "Campus-Community Partnerships: The Terms of Engagement." *Journal of Social Issues*, 2002, *58*(3), 506–516.

Community-Campus Partnerships for Health (CCHP). *Achieving the Promise of Authentic Community-Higher Education Partnerships: Community Partners Speak Out!* Retrieved February 8, 2008, from http://depts.washington.edu/ccph/pdf_files/CPS Report_final1.15.08.pdf.

City of Columbus. *Weinland Park Neighborhood Plan.* Columbus: City of Columbus, Ohio, 2006.

Creighton, S. "Universities and Communities: The Politics of Democratic Relationships." In D. W. M. Barker and D. W. Brown (eds.), *A Different Kind of Politics.* Dayton, Ohio: Kettering Foundation, 2009.

Forrest, T. M., and Goldstein, H. Weinland Park Evaluation Report. Columbus, Ohio: Ohio State University, 2010.

Hartley, M., and Hollander, E. L. "The Elusive Ideal: Civic Learning and Higher Education." In S. Fuhrman and M. Lazerson (eds.), *The Public Schools.* New York: Oxford University Press, 2005.

Harwood, R. C., and Creighton, J. A. *The Organization-First Approach: How Programs Crowd Out Community.* Bethesda, Md.: The Harwood Institute for Public Innovation, 2009.

New York State Poverty Report, 2010. Retrieved March 12, 2010, from http://www .nyscaaonline.org/PovReport/2010/2010PovReportWeb.pdf.

Peters, S. "Introduction and Overview." In S. Peters, N. R. Jordan, M. Adamek, and T. R. Alter (eds.), *Engaging Campus and Community: The Practice of Public Scholarship in the State and Land-Grant University System.* Dayton, Ohio: Kettering Foundation, 2005.

The Ithaca Campus, 2010. Retrieved May 10, 2010, from http://www.cornell.edu/ visiting/ithaca/.

Weerts, D., and Sandmann, L. "Building a Two-Way Street: Challenges and Opportunities for Community Engagement at Research Universities." *The Review of Higher Education,* 2008, *32*(1), 73–106.

White, B. P. "Bridging the High Street Divide: Community Power and the Pursuit of Democratic Partnerships Between Ohio State University and Weinland Park." Unpublished doctoral dissertation, Graduate School of Education, University of Pennsylvania, 2008.

White, B. P. *Navigating the Power Dynamics Between Institutions and Their Communities.* Dayton, Ohio: Kettering Foundation, 2009.

BYRON P. WHITE *is vice chancellor for Economic Advancement for the University System of Ohio.*

9

Academic professionals need to embrace and facilitate democratic modes of public problem solving while retaining traditional scholarly commitments.

Democratizing Academic Professionalism Inside and Out

Albert W. Dzur

Successful Failure: The Timid University

American higher education is afflicted by a condition of successful failure. In terms of academic knowledge production, America's colleges and universities are success stories, yet there is a disturbing neglect of the civic life eroding all around us. At a time of widespread public distrust of politics, institutions, and officials, a time of wicked policy problems such as overincarceration, costly health care, ineffective kindergarten through twelfth-grade education, and environmental endangerment, colleges and universities offer complacent gestures such as service-learning and civic engagement courses. They have failed more fundamentally to align organizational resources to what must be the next great academic mission: restoring American democracy.

In this chapter, I prescribe a general course of treatment for the underlying disorder: the currently inadequate connection between the culture of academic professionalism and the culture of lay citizen participation. To be sure, the university trains doctors, nurses, lawyers, public administrators, accountants, and other highly skilled workers well qualified to contribute to expert systems such as health care, criminal justice, and banking. Never has academia been more closely tied to high disciplinary standards of quality and production, or more sophisticated in its understanding of professional ethics. Such advances in this kind of professionalism, however, have failed to provide the access points that would help lay citizens constructively manage massive ongoing dysfunctions in these expert systems and thus begin to achieve greater control over public life (Giddens, 1990, p. 91).

My diagnosis and treatment plan involve a complicated, but I hope not contradictory, combination of greater self-consciousness and a more

NEW DIRECTIONS FOR HIGHER EDUCATION, no. 152, Winter 2010 © Wiley Periodicals, Inc.
Published online in Wiley Online Library (wileyonlinelibrary.com) • DOI: 10.1002/he.415

explicitly democratic commitment on and off campus. First, we need to be sober about the hidden curriculum—the technocratic administrative cultures, ineffectual institutional governance habits, and social distance between faculty and students that prevent the university from modeling a democratic way of life. Second, we should advocate university-facilitated democratic work off campus that is non-condescending, politically efficacious, yet also congruent with the university's socially unique function as a place where traditions of inquiry and creative achievement are studied, revered, and challenged.

Facing Up to the Hidden Curriculum on Campus

Nearly every semester I find an excuse to include in a syllabus the "Port Huron Statement" written by Tom Hayden and other members of the Students for a Democratic Society (Miller, 1987). This eloquent essay advocates participatory democratic American workplaces, social relations, and political institutions and explains why they would be improvements over those governed by bureaucratic and market-driven assumptions. Like a good organizer, Hayden puts the responsibility on students themselves to leverage resources exactly at the site they currently occupy. The university is not marginal to social reform, Hayden insists, it is central. Faculty take good reasons seriously and allow their classrooms to be places of critical dialogue. Such classrooms can be transformative places where repressive, hierarchical, and self-interested organizational norms are challenged. When university graduates take up positions in civil associations, corporations, and government agencies, they will slowly but surely remake them in a new image. Technical training offered at the university can be part of a process of campus socialization influenced not just by the liberal arts tradition of the centuries, but also by students themselves, who in dialogue with administrators and professors have taken that tradition into their own hands.

What is gripping about the SDS narrative is the idea that the hidden curriculum of the modern university is fundamentally democratic: deep down, the university is more egalitarian, dialogical, non-hierarchical, and free-spirited than it sometimes appears on the surface. Did I mention that I am usually the only one in the room that finds this gripping? The reason the manifesto falls flat is not because students today care little about reforming institutions. The real problem with reading the "Port Huron Statement" today is that students recognize that deep down the contemporary university is *less* democratic than it seems on the surface and therefore it cannot be realistically seen as a platform for transformative change. Although the ideology of the university holds that it operates as a horizontal collegial organization, in contemporary reality it often has a highly unaccountable vertical management structure. Relying on private search firms, boards of trustees and regents choose top personnel like presidents and provosts with no authentic input from faculty, students, or community members. Worse

NEW DIRECTIONS FOR HIGHER EDUCATION • DOI: 10.1002/he

still, the performance of central administrators is evaluated using procedures that are often less transparent and public than in business firms. Rarely is a general sense of the faculty taken with respect to major administrative measures, whereas the most symbolic use of faculty participation—consulting the "friendlies," not the "grumpies"—is all too common.

The hidden curriculum is present, too, in the classroom and in daily faculty–student non-interactions and avoidances. Though disciplinary hyperspecialization is often cited as a barrier between faculty and students, the more important issue is *social distance*: an inability to take responsibility for others as fellow citizens, collaborators—if only still learning—in a common public project of understanding and improving our social, political, and economic structures. Closing this distance is a matter of both professional ethics and democratic practice. In the months preceding the Iraq war and for much of the early occupation, faculty across the country wondered why their campuses were so quiet, so empty of controversy, so timid; they should have looked in the mirror for answers.

Parker Palmer urges universities to educate "a person who is not only competent in his or her discipline but has the skill and the will to deal with the institutional pathologies that threaten the profession's highest standards," one "who can confront, challenge, and help change the workplace" (Palmer, 2007). Universities must convey through their own practices that institutions are not alien bodies impervious to change, but are composed of real people with discernment and agency. What is needed, Palmer writes, is "an academic culture that invites students to find their voices about the program itself, gives them forums for speaking up, rewards rather than penalizes them for doing so, and encourages faculty and administrative responsiveness to student concerns."

What are the core ingredients of a more democratic academic culture? Power sharing requires freedom of speech, collegial respect, reciprocity, absence of hierarchy, suspicion of lock-step proceduralism, and commitment to collective decision making. I am sober about the deficiency of universities in living up to these norms. In the ongoing flurry of seemingly democratic action on campus—the committee meetings, the Web surveys, the advisory memos—we academics often miss how little impact any of this has on our organization and how few guarantees of true power sharing there are. That said, in my experience, power-sharing norms and practices are more vital in academic institutions than anywhere else. The threats facing them are the same threats found in all modern organization—bureaucracy, routinization, and autocracy—but there are strong countervailing traditions alive among academics (Blaug, 2010).

What is needed is real discussion with real faculty committees with real responsibilities. To that end, existing power-sharing institutions like the currently comatose academic senate require creative reforms to become more-equal partners. Creativity is also required for preserving what is essential for academic freedom in the tenure system, while extending its protections to instructors and lecturers. Power sharing without tenure protection is inconceivable.

The onus is on faculty, too, to recognize students as co-creators, as the future professionals and skilled workers who will either help or hinder public control over the expert systems that currently frustrate social ends. Beyond receptivity to student voice and influence in the seminar room, there is the more fundamental issue of time. Faculty must be able to devote time to each student with whom they come into dialogue in on-campus and off-campus work. Often, if not always, there is not enough time because of research or other campus obligations. If there is any hope of the university modeling a democratic space, we must find the time—fewer students per class, fewer classes per faculty member, fewer credits necessary to graduate— some kind of calculus that permits us to respect both research and students.

Democratic Work off Campus

For the university to fulfill its democratic mission of enabling people to control and humanize the forces that are currently disempowering and degrading them, faculty civic engagement off campus must be critiqued and transformed. My critique begins by highlighting the tension between an efficacious, democratic model of civic engagement and the self-understanding of many academic professionals that stresses the difference between the cognitive and creative work done at the university and the practical work done outside, emphasizes expertise and technical skills, and is characteristically apolitical. Because of this traditional professional identity, administrators and faculty often fail in three distinct ways to foster efficacious, democratic forms of civic engagement.

No stranger to such failure, I recall the shock of recognition when the first problem became clear: a newspaper picture of a well-respected natural scientist leading a service-learning group in playground cleanup at a local elementary school. In principle, an outstanding example of the university playing a role in the community, this engagement work was absurdly detached from the disciplinary knowledge and tools an academic had devoted his life to mastering. The access points to the world of complex scientific decision making he was well equipped to hold open were nowhere to be found on that playground. Such detachment from core academic strengths follows from the assumption that the specialized cognitive rationality of the university cannot be translated into the practical work needed outside.

The second kind of failure comes from the opposite direction; it is the overdeployment of expert knowledge. Even though university expertise can be surprisingly underutilized in civic projects, as in the playground example, expertise can still inject itself into engagement work methods, concepts, attitudes, and expectations that inadvertently downgrade the status of local knowledge and ability. The seemingly innocuous, but often undemocratic idea, that social problems are there to be fixed by the right application of professional knowledge and technique is hard for even the most self-reflective academics to shake. Also difficult to acknowledge is culpability for the ways that the system-world, largely constituted by knowledge and practice shaped in universities, has negatively impacted everyday life all around us. Hospitals, insurance firms, banks, courts, criminal justice programs, all led by university-trained professionals, have disempowered the lay public even as they have treated and otherwise quite expertly served individuals. Their largely closed management loops contribute to a sense that collective problems—health, safety, protections against predatory business practices—are beyond our control.

The third failure is the most difficult to see. It is the reluctance to confront and engage state power and resources, a disinclination that follows naturally from an age-old academic wariness of politics, a sense of pride in work that is independent of the often undignified domain of politicians and office-holders. Yet this proud independence has led to a shameful timidity at times like these, when the university must play a significant role in restoring democracy. Civic engagement can be counterproductive, mere group therapy, if it lets public officials, agencies, and institutions off the hook. Modern power is incredibly slippery, as Zygmunt Bauman has noted by drawing attention to the "shedding of responsibility" among officials, managers, and citizens themselves. Modern carelessness for those suffering from inadequate and inhumane social policy is a function neither of innate self-interest nor of improper socialization, but rather of forces that structure social life such that links to others and our responsibility for them are invisible (Bauman, 2000, pp. 87, 92). Simply put, the university cannot be neutral about the failings of our political system when the stakes for human suffering are so high.

All our major institutions and systems are in crisis—health care, criminal justice, and finance to name three. Though academics have a role in assisting in community work, they must also somehow engage the state in confronting the forces energetically destabilizing our communities. As this chapter goes to print, many Gulf Coast colleges and universities are engaged in the massive environmental cleanup demanded by the British Petroleum (BP) oil spill. Teams of service learners are devoting weeks and months of labor to this crucially important cause. As important is another kind of effort: catalyzing the scrutiny, analysis, and, ultimately, political action that can provoke reform of the state's environmental regulatory apparatus. Without the state's oversight role performed adequately, even the most extensive university civic engagement efforts will have limited long-term impact. Nevertheless, as Harry Boyte (2004, Chapter 5) has argued so persuasively, there is much academic professionals can do to collaborate with citizens as they struggle to hold managers and officials accountable.

Collaborative democratic work involving academics and communities knows when to pressure an agency, knows when to work with and when to agitate state powers to regulate a corporate actor or protect a communal space. Therefore, although we should not disparage playground or coastal cleanup projects if they serve as access points into the municipal, state, and federal agencies that impact our lives, if they fail to do so and thus remain self-contained service projects, then hope for real efficacy at a time of diffuse public responsibility is lost.

By recognizing and avoiding these three kinds of failure, the university shakes itself free of the institutional timidity that has marked its relationship with the public world for the last generation. As faculty civic engagement work becomes more democratic, it also becomes more congruent with what academic professionalism does best, more transformative of those things it does poorly, and more efficacious in these slippery late-modern times.

"Dangerous Outposts of a Humane Civilization": Modeling the Ethics and Practice of Democracy

Remodeling academic work on and off campus would revolutionize how we make manifest our professionalism in a world where it is often difficult to find our bearings. Thankfully, a more democratic form of academic professionalism recognizes the shared nature of these significant responsibilities and takes stock of the resources we already have at our disposal: the existing academic traditions of collective work, intellectual achievement, workplace autonomy, and commitment to social betterment on campus as well as the current momentum toward more-concrete public purposes off campus. An academic professionalism symbiotic with democracy remains committed to the socially unique roles of studying, revering, and challenging traditions of inquiry and creative achievement, but enlists more supporters, exercises these roles more efficaciously, and thus links the sometimes solitary life of the mind to what Hannah Arendt (1963, p. 127) called the pursuit of public happiness, a link that makes this life worth thinking and living.

Dewey called for schools to be "dangerous outposts of a humane civilization" (1922, p. 334). We can see what he means when we consider David Cooper's experience "democratizing the classroom" in the Department of Rhetoric and American Studies at Michigan State University, using a "deliberative pedagogy. . . where the learning ethos of the classroom—syllabus construction and management, assignments, assessment, heuristics, architecture, everything—is modeled after a public forum, and my role as teacher becomes that of a moderator and my students become agents and participants in the productive public work of the course" (Cooper, 2008, pp. 126, 138–139). He helped his students become co-creators of their education, while also catalyzing connections between his classes and the public world. In one, students worked in nonprofit organizations and took up responsibility for some of the public writing needed to advance organizational goals. Students "collected and analyzed examples of public writing," focusing attention on "which forms of discourse were best suited to an agency or organization's public agenda, what messages were being communicated, what positions advocated, and at which registers of the public sphere the messages were aimed (local, regional, national)" (Cooper, 2008, pp. 122–123). They also worked on public communication efforts in conjunction with the Michigan House of Representatives. What is exciting about such an example is how the traditional academic subject, in this case skilled, professional writing, is not diluted by a community-based project, but enhanced. There is a gain in both academic and civic capacity among Cooper's students, as they hold themselves to the high standards of both worlds.

Many other examples could be drawn from a wide range of institutions across the country (see Barker and Brown, 2009). From liberal arts colleges to major research universities, there is a growing sense that we need to move beyond symbolic and comfortable kinds of civic engagement, that for such work to be meaningful many facets of university life and academic professional identity itself must also be made vulnerable to transformative change. More-democratic academic professionals are becoming central to the next form of university life (see Dzur, 2008). They are building the capacity of both students and faculty to reshape the public world and they do so by drawing on the peculiar strengths that can only be found in the university.

References

Arendt, H. *On Revolution.* New York: Penguin, 1963.

Barker, D.W.M., and Brown, D. W. (eds.). *A Different Kind of Politics: Readings on the Role of Higher Education and Democracy.* Dayton, Ohio: Kettering Foundation, 2009.

Bauman, Z. "Ethics of Individuals." *Canadian Journal of Sociology,* 2000, 25, 83–96.

Blaug, R. *How Power Corrupts: Cognition and Democracy in Organisations.* London: Macmillan, 2010.

Boyte, H. *Everyday Politics: Reconnecting Citizens and Public Life.* Philadelphia: University of Pennsylvania Press, 2004.

Cooper, D. C. "Four Seasons of Deliberative Learning in a Department of Rhetoric and American Studies." In J. R. Dedrick, L. Grattan, and H. Dienstfrey (eds.), *Deliberation and the Work of Higher Education: Innovations for the Classroom, the Campus, and the Community.* Dayton, Ohio: Kettering Foundation, 2008.

Dewey, J. "Education as Politics" (1922). In J. A. Boydston (ed.), *John Dewey: The Middle Works, 1899–1924.* (Vol. 13). Carbondale, Ill.: Southern Illinois University Press, 1986.

Dzur, A. W. *Democratic Professionalism: Citizen Participation and the Reconstruction of Professional Ethics, Identity, and Practice.* University Park, Penn.: Penn State University Press, 2008.

Giddens, A. *The Consequences of Modernity.* Stanford, Calif.: Stanford University Press, 1990.

Miller, J. *"Democracy Is in the Streets": From Port Huron to the Siege of Chicago.* New York: Simon and Schuster, 1987.

Palmer, P. "A New Professional: The Aims of Education Revisited." *Change,* 2007 (Nov/Dec), 27–32.

ALBERT W. DZUR *is an associate professor in the Political Science and Philosophy Departments at Bowling Green State University.*

NEW DIRECTIONS FOR HIGHER EDUCATION • DOI: 10.1002/he

Institutional leaders, faculty, students, and the public need a better understanding of why academic freedom is essential to student learning and to a democracy characterized by open, reasoned, and vigorous political discourse.

The Politics of Academic Freedom

Nancy L. Thomas

In 2004, faculty member John Yoo returned to his tenured position at the University of California, Berkeley after serving from 2001–2003 in the Office of Legal Counsel at the U.S. Department of Justice. While there, he wrote several now-infamous memoranda that provided legal justification for detention and extreme interrogation techniques (Jaschik, 2008). These memoranda drew sharp public scrutiny after the media starting reporting on abuses and torture that the administration justified as necessary to win the "War against Terror." Several legal scholars publicly challenged Yoo's analysis. Protesters gathered outside the law school. The *New York Times* published an editorial condemning Yoo's position on torture (*New York Times*, 2008). Though not calling for his termination, the editorial noted that Yoo "inexplicably, teaches law at the University of California, Berkeley." The American Freedom Campaign began an e-mail campaign that read, "John Yoo should not only be disqualified from ever serving in government again, but he should also be prohibited from spreading his distorted view of the law and the role of lawyers to young law students. . . . He must be fired" (American Freedom Campaign, n.d.). The dean of the law school, Chris Edley, received hundreds of letters and e-mails questioning Yoo's employment. The San Francisco chapter of the Nation Lawyer's Guild wrote the University Chancellor asking for an investigation into whether Yoo violated the Faculty Code of Conduct. The matter drew ongoing commentary and debate on the *New York Times* "Room for Debate" Web page, drawing nearly 530 posts between August 20 and September 7, 2009 (*New York Times*, 2009). There is now a firejohnyoo.org Web site. On the first day of classes in August 2010, protesters mobilized outside of the law school, demanding John Yoo's termination.

John Yoo's experience pales in comparison to that of other faculty members whose research, teaching, and political speech have been the subject of proposed state legislation, government surveillance and investigations, internal university investigations, trustee calls for action, public protest, targeted

NEW DIRECTIONS FOR HIGHER EDUCATION, no. 152, Winter 2010 © Wiley Periodicals, Inc.
Published online in Wiley Online Library (wileyonlinelibrary.com) • DOI: 10.1002/he.416

Web sites, protests by irate students or the public, self-appointed "watch" groups, editorials, blogs, national media storms, radio and television talk-show rants, full-page ads in campus newspapers, e-mail campaigns, vicious name-calling, and death threats. Many who write about the barrage provide, as I have, examples of excesses stemming from all political perspectives (c.f. Gerstmann and Streb, p. 4). In the interest of transparency, I see far more critique coming from what one journalist described as a well-organized, "conservative rapid-response network" (Solow, 2004) than from those with more left-leaning views (see also Barnes, 2009).

Political pressure against higher education is nothing new but, as in the broader public square, the discourse seems to have reached a new level of invective, particularly since 9/11. Much has been written about allegations against the academy for its systemic left-leaning political bias in teaching and for protecting, under the banner of academic freedom, "dangerous" faculty out to indoctrinate students and undermine one version of the American way. Many of these strong accusations reflect not a difference of opinion, but a rejection of the very legitimacy of higher education itself. The claim is not only that the academy is too liberal; it is immoral, unpatriotic, and even dangerous to this nation. Many academics published books, articles, and op-ed pieces in the *Chronicle of Higher Education* or *InsideHigherEd.com* expressing the view that academic freedom is facing its most serious threat since the McCarthy era (Cole, 2005; Schrecker, 2006; Doumani, 2006, p. 11; Streb, 2006, p. 3).

According to researchers Smith, Mayer, and Fritschler (2008), the accusations of liberal bias in the academy lack merit. Instead, the problem is "an emerging risk-averse campus climate that threatens to impoverish the intellectual vitality" of education and inhibits political engagement (Fritschler and Smith, 2009), a viewpoint shared by other authors in this volume (see Hess and Gatti, Chapter Two, and Dzur, Chapter Nine). I can understand why academics might avoid risking choices that attract not just public attention but organized campaigns using misinformation, ridicule, and intimidation tactics. Academic freedom may ultimately protect scholarship and teaching choices, but individual scholars can be badly bloodied along the way. If, as the authors in this volume collectively argue, the academy must teach democracy's issues, principles, and practices, then being timid about tackling politically and socially controversial topics is unacceptable.

Is the prefabricated invective that dominates public life inevitable in academia as well? Are campus-watch groups, publications "outing" faculty for their political views or teaching styles, legislation, and politically motivated investigations a "new normal" for academia? We simply cannot expect embattled professors to tough it out individually. Nor does responsibility rest with the national higher education associations, even those that have issued thoughtful statements on academic freedom (Association of American Colleges and Universities [AACU], 2006; American Council on Education [ACE] 2005). The solution is certainly not to muzzle critics by drowning them out with comparable hyperbole.

New Directions for Higher Education • DOI: 10.1002/he

Students, public officials, the media, and Americans more broadly need a better understanding of why academic freedom is critical to the work of higher education, and why the work of higher education is critical to a strong democracy. With fewer than half of the nation's young people attending college, it may be that Americans do not understand or value higher education's purpose. Higher education may have devolved in the public psyche to a place where students get credentialed so that our economy grows. Although educating for individual and collective prosperity is important, higher education's responsibilities do not rest there. At their best, the nation's colleges and universities prepare students for active participation in a diverse democracy.

At the risk of sounding cliché, what is called for is a public dialogue, or at least some form of organized public engagement on academic freedom, and even higher education's role more broadly. As part of that process, the academy has some internal housekeeping to do. Academic freedom is a complex concept that warrants far more consideration than space allows in this volume (see Shiell, 2006; Strum, 2006; AACU 2006; Hamilton and Gaff, 2009; O'Neil, 2008 for excellent summaries of academic freedom's history, scope, and purpose). My goal for this chapter is to address three specific concerns: how academic freedom is framed and discussed; faculty neutrality, particularly in the classroom; and student rights. I conclude with some suggestions on how the principles and practices of deliberative democracy can foster understanding of and commitment to academic freedom.

Academic Freedom's Purpose

Much of what is said and written about academic freedom has to do with the right of professors to free inquiry that leads to the discovery and teaching of new knowledge and the truth. Although this is vitally important, we need to shift the conversation from academic freedom as an individual right to academic freedom as a collective duty, a responsibility implicit in the social contract between American higher education and democracy. It is a duty to study and teach subjects in ways that are publicly relevant and that inform and elevate the public discourse.

We can start by being more attentive to how the academy makes the case for academic freedom. Judicial recognition of academic freedom as a legal standard and constitutionally protected principle and public interest forever changed the way we talk about it.[1] In the often-referenced *Keyishian v. Board of Regents* (1967), the U.S. Court described the classroom as "the marketplace of ideas" (385 U.S. 589, 603). Justice Brennan explained, "Our Nation is deeply committed to safeguarding academic freedom, which is of transcendent value to all of us . . . That freedom is therefore a special concern of the First Amendment, which does not tolerate laws that cast a pall of orthodoxy over the classroom." American colleges and universities excel not by stamping with approval conventional social and political views. They strengthen society when they compel students to explore the complexity of subjects, analyze, critique, and deliberate when there is disagreement, and generate new ideas and solutions. Academic freedom exists so that colleges and universities *can and will* be places for the robust exchange of ideas and free expression. It is "a constitutionally significant means to a constitutionally desired end" (Barnes, 2009, p. 1468).

In describing academic freedom, we can invoke U.S. Supreme Court Chief Justice Warren's language in 1957 (*Sweezy v. State of New Hampshire*, 354 U.S. 234, 250):

> No one should underestimate the vital role in a democracy that is played by those who guide and train our youth. To impose any strait jacket upon the intellectual leaders in our colleges and universities would imperil the future of our Nation. No field of education is so thoroughly comprehended by man that new discoveries cannot yet be made. Particularly is that true in the social sciences, where few, if any, principles are accepted as absolutes. Scholarship cannot flourish in an atmosphere of suspicion and distrust. Teachers and students must always remain free to inquire, to study and to evaluate, to gain new maturity and understanding; otherwise our civilization will stagnate and die.

Perhaps Berkeley Law School Dean Chris Edley (2008) offered the best rationale for academic freedom:

> [John Yoo] enjoys not only security of employment and academic freedom, but also First Amendment and Due Process rights . . . It seems we do need regular reminders: These protections, while not absolute, are nearly so because they are essential to the excellence of American universities and the progress of ideas. Indeed, in Berkeley's classrooms and courtyards our community argues about the legal and moral issues with the intensity and discipline these crucial issues deserve. Those who prefer to avoid these arguments—be they left or right or lazy—will not find Berkeley or any other truly great law school a wholly congenial place to study. For that we make no apology.

Embracing this perspective on academic freedom strengthens the democratic purposes of higher education and helps to protect academic freedom from those who seek to erode it in service to a political agenda.

Neutrality

Many academics dismissed the attacks by the likes of David Horowitz as coming from extremists with their own political agenda. That may be, but we need to take seriously the principle of neutrality. Several studies of faculty attitudes indicate that a majority—slightly more than 60 percent—of college faculty members lean to the left ideologically (Smith, Mayer, and Fritschler, 2008, p. 74). These numbers change dramatically when broken down by discipline. For example, the most liberal departments are English

(85%) and foreign language and sociology (80%); the least liberal are economics (23%), agriculture (31%), and business (34%). Faculties are made up mostly of Democrats (56%) and Independents (30%), with Republicans making up only 14% (Smith, Mayer, and Fritschler, 2008, p. 78).

Do professors indoctrinate students or even demonstrate bias in their classrooms? Seventy-five percent of faculty surveyed (both liberal and conservative-leaning) felt that there is no significant pattern of bias on their campuses (Smith, Mayer, and Fritschler, 2008, p. 83), but that may be because academics avoid politics. Contrary to conventional wisdom, most faculty members keep politics out of their classrooms, and those that do talk politics are not inclined to let their students know how they feel about an issue (p. 84).

It is unrealistic to expect professors to *be* neutral, but they do need to *act* neutrally in the classroom, to be objective and fair about a topic. (When they are out in the public arena, they have the same rights as any other citizen.) The challenge here is largely one of *process*: who gets called on, how to balance individual and group needs, how to manage personal beliefs and opinions, how to broaden a discussion when there is inadequate diversity in perspectives among the students.The job of a professor is to encourage independent thinking and create safe spaces for free expression and deliberation. It is to provide students with opportunities to examine public problems carefully and identify or craft well-reasoned solutions after a respectful airing of diverse perspectives.

The challenge is also one of content, and expert knowledge and opinion count. A desired learning outcome should not be to indoctrinate students or manipulate public opinion, but of course, the lines are almost never this bright. Academics are on the front line of many significant normative debates in society. Some political questions are central to a discipline, and they may demand a definitive stance (e.g., what causes the economy to grow, whether democracy is the best political system, climate change, new forms of energy). As researchers, discover new knowledge and support legitimate perspectives with empirical evidence. As teachers, the goal is to provide a context for a robust exchange of ideas, and those exchanges will inevitably influence learning, career and personal choices such as voting, judging the conduct and decisions of public officials, and public problem solving.

Progressive thinking may be viewed as subversive or radical, but challenges to a professor's legitimacy as a researcher and teacher are best left to peers and others with relevant knowledge and training. Academics appropriately resist challenges to their scholarship and teaching when they feel that the pressure is politically motivated.

Student Rights

Much of the recent controversy concerns faculty–student dynamics. Do students have the right to refuse an assignment or to learn a topic if they believe a professor teaches from a biased perspective? Generally, the answer to these and similar questions is no. Students can and should be required to articulate and defend their positions, and it is entirely appropriate for a professor to challenge strongly held viewpoints, even if the student suspects (or even knows) that the professor feels just as strongly. Students do not have the right to avoid an educational experience because they are upset or their perspectives have been challenged by legitimate facts and ideas. Except in rare circumstances, they cannot refuse to study a topic, even if it is against their religious beliefs.

It is entirely appropriate for a professor to insist upon reason in a classroom setting, but s/he needs to consider who decides what is reasonable and whether their standards are linked to the norms established by those with positional power or authority. Faculty should not quash dissenting perspectives under the guise of maintaining classroom order.

Students do not have the right to disrupt the educational process or obstruct teaching and learning. Students generally can challenge the views expressed by faculty, institutional leaders, peers, and guests both in and beyond the classroom, and institutions and faculty have the right to insist upon evidence, respect and other rules for discourse, and reasonable time, place, and manner restrictions, as long as those rules are not tantamount to censorship.

Professors can insist on respect and civility in the classroom, and they should respond in kind. Professors must treat students with respect, but that can mean different things to different people. (Chapter One examines the complexity of civility as a rule for engagement.) Common sense should prevail: professors cannot disparage, harass, humiliate, or exploit students. Some courts have concluded that professors cannot be vulgar, although others have protected obscenity in certain circumstances.

Again, the lines are not always clear. One person's Socratic method is another person's harassment. Members of a classroom or campus activities should collaboratively establish and periodically affirm ground rules in advance of any discussion. Students can be held to higher standards for discourse than are currently modeled in some political arenas.

Allegations of "hate speech" should be managed on a case-by-case basis and both faculty and campuses should avoid preemptive, blanket restrictions. This topic, of course, could be its own book. As a society, we simply must find ways to challenge ideas without personal attacks, and campuses should be communities that encourage and model civil discourse, not by censoring uncivil speech but by exposing and critiquing it.

Establishing Democratic Culture and Habits of Deliberative Democracy

Members of a campus community can take cues from deliberative democracy advocates and orient teaching and learning to the democratic practices and principles mentioned throughout this volume (see the Clark University case study, Chapter Three, for example). These practices—dialogue, informed deliberation, analysis, and problem solving—and their guiding principles—inclusion, reason, respect, neutrality, and collegiality—are critical to a strong democracy *and* to the academy as it meets its obligations under its social contract with democracy. Campuses miss the point if they continue to offer the typical, predominantly passive venues—debates, presentations, public lectures, panel discussions followed by Q&A or short roundtable discussions, focus groups, and apolitical service. These are not *deliberative* settings. The campus culture should reflect exemplary principles and practices in democratic dialogue and public deliberation.

My own apprehension stems from the conundrum higher education faces. Academic work—inquiry, study, critique, deliberation, and problem solving—is inherently *progressive*. Shining a spotlight on pressing ethical, social, political, and economic problems in society, not simply as a proverbial academic exercise but as a step toward social change, is the job. To many, that implies an activist role and even a *partisan* agenda, so the public pushback is likely to be not only against scholarly conclusions (and the fact that they are taught), but against the very idea that this is the academy's "place." Our challenge is to communicate publicly how teaching and learning about public problems and their solutions is in the public's best interest, and why that is best accomplished when faculty have the freedom to do so in nonpartisan ways and without political interference.

Berkeley Law Dean Chris Edley suggested, "we do need regular reminders" about the scope and purpose of academic freedom. How do we do that? I am heartened by the promising developments in public discourse and successful experiments in inclusive, reasoned, respectful dialogue and deliberation. There is no reason why those principles and practices cannot be applied to teaching and learning political controversies and to bolstering public understanding and commitment to academic freedom. With the exception of extremists who steadfastly employ divisive, vitriolic diatribe to get their way, Americans want more informed, open, and civil discourse and productive problem solving in public life about pressing social and political problems (Shea, 2009). They should expect it in higher education as well.

Note

1. Academic Freedom is an amorphous concept in legal jurisprudence. I am not arguing that we can count on the courts to protect all faculty speech from political pressure. Indeed, the U.S. Constitution only limits the actions of the *state*, not *individuals* (e.g., bloggers, citizen watch groups). Further, the constitutionally protected right to academic freedom (distinguished here from academic freedom as a professional standard or contract right) is an *institutional* right enjoyed by faculty members as agents of the university. Finally, academic freedom is not absolute.

References

American Council on Education, "Statement on Academic Rights and Responsibilities." Released June 23, 2005. Retrieved January 7, 2011 at http://www.acenet.edu/AM/Template.cfm?Section=Search&template=/CM/ContentDisplay.cfm&ContentID=10672.

Association of American Colleges and Universities [AACU]. "Academic Freedom & Educational Responsibility." *Liberal Education*, 2006, 92(2), 6.

American Freedom Campaign. "Tell the Dean of UC Berkeley School of Law to Fire John Yoo." Retrieved September 3, 2010, from http://salsa.democracyinaction.org/o/2165/t/1027/campaign.jsp?campaign_KEY=24188.

Barnes, R. D. "Natural Legal Guardians of Judicial Independence and Academic Freedom." *Fordham Law Review*, 2009, 77, 1453–1477.

Cole, J. R. "The New McCarthyism." *The Chronicle Review*, 2005, 52(3), B7.

Doumani, B. (ed.). *Academic Freedom after September 11*. New York: Zone Books, 2006.

Edley, C. "The Torture Memos and Academic Freedom," Memorandum dated April 10, 2008. Retrieved January 7, 2011, from http://www.law.berkeley.edu/news/2008/edley041008.html.

Fritschler, A. L., and Smith, B.L.R. "The New Climate of Timidity on Campuses." *Chronicle of Higher Education*, 2009, 55(23), A80.

Gerstmann, E., and Streb, M. J. *Academic Freedom at the Dawn of a New Century*. Stanford, Calif.: Stanford University Press, 2006.

Hamilton, N. W., and Gaff, J. G. *The Future of the Professoriate: Academic Freedom, Peer Review, and Shared Governance*. Washington, D.C.: Association of American Colleges and Universities, 2009.

Jaschik, S. "Torture and Tenure." *Inside HigherEd*. April 14, 2008. Retrieved September 3, 2010, from http://www.insidehighered.com/news/2008/04/14/yoo.

Keyishian v. Board of Regents, 385 U.S. 589 (1967).

New York Times. "There Were Orders to Follow." Editorial, April 4, 2008. Retrieved August 25, 2010, from http://www.nytimes.com/2008/04/04/opinion/04fri1.html.

New York Times. "Torture and Academic Freedom." A "Room for Debate" ongoing commentary. August 9, 2009. Retrieved September 5, 2010, from http://roomfordebate.blogs.nytimes.com/2009/08/20/torture-and-academic-freedom/.

O'Neil, R. M. *Academic Freedom in the Wired World: Political Extremism, Corporate Power, and the University*. Cambridge, Mass.: Harvard University Press, 2008.

Schrecker, E. "Worse than McCarthy." *The Chronicle Review*, 2006, 52(23), B20.

Shea, D. M. "Nastiness, Name-calling & Negativity—The Allegheny College Survey of Civility and Compromise in American Politics." 2009. Retrieved June 19, 2010, from http://sitesmedia.s3.amazonaws.com/civility/files/2010/04/AlleghenyCollegeCivilityReport2010.pdf.

Shiell, T. "Three Conceptions of Academic Freedom." In E. Gertsmann and M. J. Streb (eds.), *Academic Freedom at the Dawn of a New Century*. Stanford: Stanford University Press, 2006, pp. 17–40.

Smith, B. L. R., Mayer, J. D., and Fritschler, A. L. *Closed Minds? Politics and Ideology in American Universities*, Washington, D.C.: The Brookings Institution, 2008.

Solow, B. "Academia Under Siege." *Independence Online*, March 31, 2004. Retrieved August 25, 2010, from http://www.indyweek.com/indyweek/academia-under-siege/Content?oid=1191788.

Streb, M. J. "The Reemergency of the Academic Freedom Debate," in E. Gertsmann and M. J. Streb (eds.) *Academic Freedom at the Dawn of a New Century*. Stanford: Stanford Universitiy Press, 2006, pp. 3–16.

Strum, P. "Why Academic Freedom? The Theoretical and Constitutional Context." In B. Doumani (ed.), *Academic Freedom after September 11*. New York: Zone Books, 2006, pp. 143–172.

Sweezy v. State of New Hampshire, 354 U.S. 234 (1957).

NANCY L. THOMAS *directs the Democracy Imperative at the University of New Hampshire and is a senior associate with Everyday Democracy.*

NEW DIRECTIONS FOR HIGHER EDUCATION • DOI: 10.1002/he

11

Strategies for moving closer to effective forms of shared governance, using deliberative approaches that sustain faculty authority over the academic mission.

Practicing What We Preach: Democratic Practices in Institutional Governance

Bruce L. Mallory

In fall 1997, the faculty, staff, and students at the University of New Hampshire (Durham, New Hampshire) were consumed with a divisive and public debate over the limits of academic freedom, the consequences of provocative pedagogy, and claims about the "chilly climate" for women students in some classroom situations. The debate had been precipitated by complaints made by several women enrolled in a class with a male professor who was alleged to have used sexual references and metaphors in his lectures. The professor did not deny his use of provocative language and further claimed that some degree of discomfort was a necessary tool to heighten attention and create a lively classroom atmosphere. Thus began an intense process of hearings, grievances, and public debate about how to balance the principles of academic freedom against the need to create a nonthreatening learning environment for the full range of students at the university.

For a while, the debate followed the predictable path of letters to the campus newspaper, defense of the professor's right to determine what to say and how to say it in his classroom, charges that the campus had a general problem of gender discrimination and harassment, and ultimately litigation. In the end, a settlement was produced that involved the departure of the professor from the university, but that did not resolve any of the core questions that had arisen about academic freedom and the need for a safe learning environment for all students. This inconclusive ending led to a call for a campuswide dialogue on the relationship between academic freedom and the increasing awareness that some students felt uncomfortable and even harassed during class discussions as a function of their social identity.

NEW DIRECTIONS FOR HIGHER EDUCATION, no. 152, Winter 2010 © Wiley Periodicals, Inc.
Published online in Wiley Online Library (wileyonlinelibrary.com) • DOI: 10.1002/he.417

The call for dialogue resulted in the first use at the university of an explicit effort to address contested issues through facilitated, small group "study circles" intended to engage the full range of constituencies in defining the scope of the problem, analyze its various manifestations, and produce specific guidelines and policies. At the time, I had been applying the study circle model in off-campus, community contexts in which citizens were facing highly charged debates over public education issues (including funding decisions, curriculum matters, and local governance). As a faculty member and recently appointed dean of the graduate school, I was seen as someone who could bring both a faculty and administrator's perspective to the issue, in combination with my experience in fostering deliberative practices. The campuswide study circles of faculty, staff, and students produced a set of recommendations that were incorporated into the university's policy documents and laid the groundwork for ongoing efforts to use deliberative processes in matters that required collegial and inclusive shared governance.

This chapter examines the principles of shared governance and shared leadership, including the obstacles to achieving those ideals. It then offers examples of deliberation and dialogue in concrete governance challenges. The chapter concludes with a series of questions that a campus might use to assess its own shared governance practices and to determine how deliberative approaches can be utilized to create a more democratic, participatory community. Essentially, the intent of the chapter is to connect the democratic purposes of higher education—to produce graduates who are capable of functioning as effective citizens in a pluralistic democracy—with the ways in which we govern ourselves. If we do not practice what we preach, we cannot expect our students to learn and be committed to creating the kind of effective, pluralistic democracy that is arguably one of the core purposes of higher education in the United States.

Shared Governance: An Elusive Goal?

An important starting point for understanding what is meant by shared governance is the "Statement on Government of Colleges and Universities" jointly developed by the American Association of University Professors (AAUP), the American Council on Education, and the Association of Governing Boards of Universities and Colleges (AAUP, 1966/1990). The Statement as a whole is predicated on the belief that "a college or university in which all the components are aware of their interdependence, of the usefulness of communication among themselves, and of the force of joint action will enjoy increased capacity to solve educational problems." The Statement explicates three major domains of "joint effort"—general educational policy, internal operations, and external relations. Joint effort in this sense refers to the "inescapable interdependence among governing board, administration, faculty, students, and others."

NEW DIRECTIONS FOR HIGHER EDUCATION • DOI: 10.1002/he

In my work as a dean and then provost, I had the opportunity to develop a set of principles regarding shared governance, through a series of conversations with the faculty senate. These working guidelines, adopted jointly by the administration and senate, included the following:

1. Shared governance is a "best operating practice," grounded in continuing, open, and reciprocal dialogue. Continual consultation with the appropriate constituencies builds mutual trust and goodwill.
2. Shared governance asks that we see things from all sides, not just our own, and that we "put ourselves in the others' shoes."
3. Anticipatory approaches will be more likely to result in successful shared governance than after-the-fact discussions. It is important to communicate and consult regardless of circumstance.
4. To inform is not to consult; consultations require informed participants who respect historical and present contexts.
5. Shared governance implies that all "sides" must continue to communicate even under the most difficult circumstances.
6. Sufficient time for shared governance on particular issues should be allocated in order to recognize the urgency, circumstances, and potential long-term impacts of decisions.
7. Shared governance requires clear communication of multiple perceptions about causes and remedies of any given challenge. An accurate definition and specification of the problem are essential components to guide decisions.
8. Shared governance may include processes of shared implementation in addition to shared decision making.
9. Shared governance requires a budget system that serves academic priorities rather than defining those priorities.
10. Shared governance principles should be explicit, published, honored, and revisited on a regular basis.

This set of principles is consistent with Young's (1997) delineation of values that promote scholarship as well as democracy. His framing is useful in that it can align the promotion of scholarship with democratic and participatory (shared) governance practices. Young proposes that the underlying values necessary for effective shared governance include a belief in the value of service (what I would call an ethic of participation), truth (or a commitment to the use of empirical data and the rational analysis of those data), freedom (in the traditional academic sense of unfettered inquiry and critique), equality (a democratic ideal in which each voice in the academy counts even as status differences may imply differential degrees of authority), and community. It is this last value that, in my view, represents a necessary condition for effective shared governance and can be directly fostered through deliberative practices.

We could state that shared governance is about learning, development, and enhancing the lives of the members of our community, which in turn

NEW DIRECTIONS FOR HIGHER EDUCATION • DOI: 10.1002/he

leads to a strengthening of the community itself. In a recent article on the role of public reason in a democracy, Thomas (2007, p. 9) wrote, "Communities come together to frame a conflict, issue, or problem. Members of a community listen to each other's perspectives and ideas. They study in more depth what they do not know. They discuss the choices and weigh competing values and interests. Ideally, the community comes to accept refined versions of one or more solutions that are collectively viewed as reasonable. Decisions may not make everyone happy—they may not reflect a consensus—but they do reflect the reasoned overall will of the community."

Each person, each citizen if you will, contributes to this value no matter where she or he works in the university. As such, we all have responsibilities as community members to behave toward others as we would want them to behave toward us. The golden rule for the person-within-community, a key ingredient to successful deliberation, is also a necessary condition for the successful practice of shared governance.

Shared Leadership

The principles of shared governance require an understanding of the concept of *shared leadership*. Whether we serve on department committees or as department chairs or deans or senators or as a provost or trustee, we each operate with limited, sometimes conflicting data that can serve as the basis for short-term decisions and long-term strategies. And we only see the university from the particular vantage point of our department, college, or office. This means that we must join with others who stand at different vantage points to compare and aggregate data, perceptions, and theories to arrive at shared understandings and common purpose—to triangulate our observations, as it were. This social constructionist paradigm (Bess and Dee, 2008) of deliberative and shared leadership aligns with the general democratic and participatory principles we raised in the discussion of shared governance.

Shared leadership requires what Ponder and McCauley (2006) label as relational competencies—"those skills, abilities, and mindsets that enable leaders to build trust, confidence, and fairness in their relationships with a diverse set of individuals and communities" (p. 225). Through our relationships with others, both within our local disciplinary neighborhoods and in the commons, we negotiate the sometimes treacherous and shifting paths of reality, facts, perceptions, data, values, and ideologies—no simple process among people who have been both trained and socialized to dispute the given and ask hard questions. This constant process of negotiating difficult and dynamic paths is informed by the important distinction between management and leadership. Bennis and Nanus (1985) make the distinction between management and leadership; the former is about doing things right while the latter is about doing the right things. Managers sustain the norms and rules of an organization. Leaders are expected to inspire and originate.

Further, they see shared governance as a set of interdependencies and mutual responsibilities among trustees, administration, staff, faculty, and students. One way to build such shared understandings is by creating the deliberative time and space necessary to work through issues of trust, competing information, and sometimes divergent values.

Creating a Culture of Deliberation

"There is little in place to encourage healthy resolution of conflict between and often within departments." "The pace of life impacts our ability and willingness to work through conflict." "More than anything, people want to feel included. They want an opportunity to voice their opinion BEFORE a decision has been made, not when it's a done deal or on its way to being one." These quotes were collected at the end of a campuswide study circle at the University of New Hampshire in 2003, framed as "University or Polyversity? The Promise of Conflict at UNH." The study circles were organized after what seemed to be an unusual confluence of challenges, including a prolonged faculty contract dispute, a series of campus celebrations that turned into very uncivil disturbances, several alcohol-related assaults, and other incidents that required some degree of crisis management. In this case, a deliberative process was used to address cultural issues that had strained the whole community. It was a way for the community to pause, reflect, and consider how we might anticipate and respond to crises in the future. All constituencies were involved, including local city councilors, police, and merchants.

Another example of deliberation as a means to foster shared governance at UNH occurred in 2004, in a round of study circles on "The Compelling Interest of Diversity: How Should UNH Meet Its Educational and Civic Responsibilities to Foster an Inclusive Campus Community?" This project was a response to the *Grutter v. Bollinger* 2003 U.S. Supreme Court decision *Grutter v. Bollinger*, 539 US 306 (2003). Our goal was to create formal statements of purpose and policy that would guide the university's increasing commitments to diversity while reflecting directly the opportunities and constraints articulated in the Court's majority decision. At the end of the process, participants called for more systematic, strategic, and sustained efforts at creating a more inclusive community; greater efforts to recruit and retain diverse faculty, staff, and students; the articulation of an institutional commitment to diversity consistent with the *Grutter* decision; and regular data collection related to diversity initiatives that could be used to improve future efforts.

There have been several other rounds of deliberations at UNH, on issues related to "responsible celebrations," the role of alcohol in the community and its impact on behavior and academic performance, and shared governance. In addition, since 2005 we have held year-long university dialogues on globalization, energy, poverty, democracy, health, and the age of digital information. In this way, all members of the community experience democratic practices in governance processes, community-university relationships, and curricular as well as co-curricular activities. If authentic deliberation is to become a part of the culture of a college or university, its use across constituencies and functions increases the likelihood that it will be consequential and sustained.

Our attempts to create a more deliberative and democratic culture has been challenged by the entrenched characteristics of campus culture with which readers of this volume are quite familiar. For example, Al Dzur's chapter describes symbolic uses of consultation and transparency as a poor substitute for authentic participatory governance. He also acknowledges the "disciplinary hyper-specialization" that sustains intellectual walls that easily morph into structural and communicative barriers. In a report published in 2008, William Leach's analysis of shared governance offers a detailed framing of challenges to effective shared governance. Among the numerous barriers he describes, those most salient to this chapter include disagreements over what shared governance is and should look like, a mutual lack of trust between administrators and faculty (sharpened by the clash between managerial and academic values), the disenfranchisement of part-time faculty and the lack of governance structures where their voices can be heard, and the "prevalent underperformance" of faculty senates. Thus, efforts to create more deliberative forms of governance might start with conversations explicitly about these barriers, even before attempting to instill more collaborative practices.

Where to Begin?

Before moving toward more deliberative, participatory approaches to governance, a number of self-reflective questions might be asked to assess an institution's readiness. The process of answering such questions can itself be a way of safely practicing deliberation before applying it to high stakes issues such as academic freedom or affirmative action policies. A process of self-reflection might include the following questions:

- How can consultation and collaboration be truly mutual or equitable when one side has supervisory, financial, and infrastructure power over the other?
- Faculty senates are representative forms of democracy. Why do they have such bad reputations for effectiveness in general? Are they the right forums for deliberation?
- What alternative forums for deliberation exist or could be created, while still respecting the formal authority of senates and other existing governance bodies? How can alternative forums be legitimized and heard?
- What is the difference between faculty senates and academic senates? How can one or the other foster collegiality?

- What are the rewards for engaging in participatory democratic practices in university governance?
- How does the presence of a faculty union affect shared governance practices?
- Has there been an effort to delineate spheres of primary authority (curriculum, standards, planning, finances, mission, etc.)?
- Who sets agendas, fosters new initiatives, and designs assessment and feedback mechanisms?
- What is the culture for decision making (top down, adversarial, collaborative, bottom-up, bureaucratic, ad hoc)?
- Is there a shared sense of mission and direction?

These kinds of questions are too often left unanswered, even though they may be an implicit part of the conversations and debates that constitute efforts at shared governance. The effort to open up the campus to such questions can be an important beginning to building the kind of trust and social capital necessary for effective, collegial governance. Moreover, we can demonstrate to our students that we are willing to practice what we preach about the value of an inclusive, pluralistic democracy. That would justify the risks in taking on the questions that others and I have raised throughout this volume.

References

American Association of University Professors. *Statement on Government of Colleges and Universities.* Washington, D.C.: American Association of University Professors, 1966/1990.

Bennis, W., and Nanus, J. *Leaders: New Strategies for Taking Charge.* New York: Harper and Row, 1985.

Bess, J. L., & Dee, J. R. *Understanding College and University Organization: Theories for Effective Policy and Practice Volume 1: The State of the System.* Sterling Va.: Stylus, 2008.

Leach, W. D. *Shared Governance in Higher Education: Structural and Cultural Responses to a Changing National Climate.* Sacramento, Calif.: Center for Collaborative Policy, California State University, 2008.

Ponder, K. M., and McCauley, C. D. "Leading in the Unique Character of Academe: What It Takes." In D. G. Brown (ed.), *University Presidents as Moral Leaders. The American Council on Education Praeger Series on Higher Education.* Westport, Conn.: Praeger Publishers, 2006, p. 211.

Thomas, N. L. "Educating for Deliberative Democracy: The Role of Public Reason and Reasoning." *Journal of College and Character*, 2007, 11(7), 9.

Young, R. B. *No Neutral Ground: Standing by the Values We Prize in Higher Education.* San Francisco: Jossey-Bass, 1997.

BRUCE L. MALLORY *is professor of education and former provost and executive vice president of the University of New Hampshire.*

12

Where do we go from here? Next steps for higher education.

Higher Education's Democratic Imperative

Nancy L. Thomas, Matthew Hartley

Last summer, the Democracy Imperative and the Deliberative Democracy Consortium, two national networks linking academics and deliberative democracy practitioners, hosted a national conference, No Better Time: Promising Opportunities in Deliberative Democracy for Educators and Practitioners (*No Better Time*, 2010). Over 250 civic leaders, community organizers, faculty, academic leaders, foundation representatives, and students met at the University of New Hampshire (Durham, New Hampshire) to discuss higher education's role in strengthening democracy in the twenty-first century.

The conference was designed to encourage an exchange of ideas among an almost even mix of academics and practitioners who co-created the agenda. Participants proposed and organized "learning exchanges," two-and-a-half-hour sessions for democratic dialogue and action planning. The process produced fifty learning exchanges on critical public issues (e.g., the economy, poverty); promising practices for effective deliberation (e.g., which deliberative approaches might be used in various settings, approaches to values inquiry); curriculum and program development; challenges and opportunities in the field and on campus (e.g., the risk-averse culture of the academy, the emergence of e-democracy, integrating advocacy and deliberation, and the difficulty in finding language that adequately describes this work). After the conference, session leaders reflected on their experiences by completing worksheets and answering a survey. Drawing from these sources, the conference organizers identified priorities for the field and for higher education. Simply stated, higher education has a unique opportunity to establish and assert itself in the movement to strengthen twenty-first century democracy. Collectively, the authors in this book make compelling cases for specific actions, such as addressing the values tensions inherent in advocating for

NEW DIRECTIONS FOR HIGHER EDUCATION, no. 152, Winter 2010 © Wiley Periodicals, Inc.
Published online in Wiley Online Library (wileyonlinelibrary.com) • DOI: 10.1002/he.418

Table 12.1 Five Ways Higher Education Can Strengthen Democracy

1. Teach civics
2. Teach current political controversies
3. Teach democratic skills
4. Establish deliberative spaces for public problem solving
5. Model democracy

civility (Chapter One), teaching politics (Chapter Two), serving as partners in and catalysts for community development (Chapters Five and Six), redirecting the research agenda (Chapter Seven), staying attentive to community–university dynamics and the realities of power and privilege (Chapter Eight) and practicing shared governance internally (Chapter Eleven). The following list reflects the insights of the authors in this volume and the *No Better Time* conference, as well as a few of our own (see Table 12.1).

#1: Teach Civics

It may seem self-evident, but one cannot be effective as a citizen if one does not understand the levers of change in a democracy. Americans need a deeper understanding of basic civics, a deficit that has been well documented (Delli Carpini and Keeter, 1997). Public Agenda (2002) optimistically reported that Americans "know it by heart," meaning that they have a general (albeit an often implicit) understanding of their basic civil liberties, rule of law, and American history. This is at best a foundation for a truly knowledgeable and active citizenry.

Studies that compare today's young people to other generational cohorts show that they are the least knowledgeable about government structure, historical events, and contemporary politics (Wichowsky, 2002). Further, efforts to prepare them to assume their civic responsibilities have fallen precipitously (Lane, 2008, 54). The drumbeat of accountability and the widespread use of high-stakes testing at the kindergarten through twelfth-grade level have driven basic areas of instruction like social studies out of the curriculum in many school districts. It falls on colleges and universities to fill these gaps.

A comprehensive review of what students should learn is a larger topic than space here allows. At the very least, Americans should know the key events in American history from which American democracy evolved. They should understand the basic workings of American democracy such as the three branches of government and the principal of checks and balances, how a bill becomes a law, and the principals of civil liberties and civil rights. They should be able answer questions such as, "What is guaranteed under the First Amendment?" "Why do we need a multiparty system?" They should be exposed to different political viewpoints and values tensions. They should examine progressive, libertarian, communitarian, conservative, and egalitarian perspectives. They should develop what Eric Lane (2008) calls "a constitutional conscience"—knowledge of the U.S. Constitution's evolution of its values of freedom, justice, and equality. They should know the difference between the Declaration of Independence, the Constitution, and the Bill of Rights.

This sort of deep understanding requires more than one required course. Relying on political science departments is inadequate because they reach only a fraction of all students, and they tend to focus on an analysis of, rather than the work of, democracy. Students need opportunities to connect theory to practice. Civic literacy needs to be an overarching learning objective and an outgrowth of an overall educational strategy that emphasizes democratic learning.

#2: Teach Current Political Controversies

Students want an education that is practical and personally relevant. It is also the case that many students have little knowledge of current events. For example, a 2009 survey of 219,864 first-year students at four-year institutions found that only 36 percent considered "keeping up to date with political affairs" an important activity (Higher Education Research Institute, 2010). Current events and contemporary public problems present rich opportunities to link disciplinary and democratic learning.

Given this state of affairs, we are struck by how few colleges and universities have made sustained, cohesive, and campuswide efforts to talk about matters of fundamental importance to our democracy. For example, the aftermath of 9/11 raised important questions about the sorts of actions that are warranted during times of national threat and how best to balance national security with civil liberties. In American history the writ of habeas corpus, a Constitutional right that protects Americans from unjustified or capricious arrest and detention, had been suspended only four times before 9/11: during the Civil War, Reconstruction, the Spanish–American War (in the Philippines), and during World War II. When it was again suspended after 9/11 for the "War on Terror," campuses remained silent. Such important matters of public policy should be discussed and debated nationally, and colleges and universities should be taking the lead to ensure this happens. The tradeoffs and values tensions that emerge in such debates need to be elaborated so that students understand that in important matters, there are rarely easy answers or "silver bullets."

#3: Teach Democratic Skills

Democracy is a practice. It is important for colleges and universities to be intentional about identifying the democratic skills they would like students to learn (much as they might identify other core skills such as critical thinking or good writing) and to develop curricular and co-curricular experiences aimed at enhancing students' proficiency in these areas.

Civic organizations have developed a range of effective approaches to democratic practice: study circles, choice work, issue framing, viewpoint learning, large- and small-group discussions, intergroup dialogue, and sustained dialogue (Heierbacher, n.d.). Of course, many faculty members will need professional development opportunities to adapt them to a classroom context. Faculty may know how to elegantly steer a class discussion around disciplinary content, but many are unsure how to deal with controversial topics or interpersonal conflicts. Faculty may need help learning how to establish ground rules for democratic deliberation, facilitate discussions about difficult topics, manage the "unexpected," and capitalize on conflict, inevitabilities in deliberative discussions.

These sorts of classroom-based experiences can also be powerfully reinforced if they are also brought into the co-curriculum. Residence halls can be creatively reimagined as civic spheres where students collectively make decisions about how they want to live as a community. Many colleges and universities have established learning communities where groups of students and faculty learn and live together for a year—often these communities have democratic themes. These offer important opportunities for students to develop their democratic selves. Taken together, curricular and co-curricular efforts can be ideal venues for democratic education and engagement.

As noted in the editor's opening chapter, the goal of skill building needs to include increasing broader citizen, not just student, capacity for effective public participation. Because only about half of young adults attend college, the solution has to be more effective partnerships between the academy, communities, and civic organizations skilled in deliberative processes, partnerships that will get skill levels to a scale that we need to benefit all communities, not just those with a high percentage of college-educated residents.

Participants at the *No Better Time* conference also emphasized the special need for democratic skill development among two particular groups: teachers and public officials. Here, the task might be to specifically reach out to these public servants for inclusion in learning exchanges, described below.

#4: Establish Deliberative Spaces for Public Problem Solving

Colleges and universities are ideally situated to serve as sites for the work of democracy and public problem solving. They have the physical resources to convene students, faculty, staff, civic leaders, government officials, and everyday citizens. They have a wealth of disciplinary expertise within their walls and have close ties with individuals and organizations in the community that bring many kinds of expertise and diverse perspectives to the table.

Typically, individuals on campuses conceive and host such events by selecting a topic, pulling together a panel of resident academic experts and guest speakers who frame the issue and wax eloquent for a time, followed by a Q&A session (or, if the organizers are radical, roundtable conversations). Such events are a perfectly fine means of conveying information. They are hardly models of democratic deliberation. We need to experiment with other models. The *No Better Time* conference was itself an experiment in self-organizing public space for deliberation. Conference participants proposed "learning exchanges," two-and-a-half-hour sessions where participants modeled deliberative democracy. Sessions were typically organized by an academic–practitioner team; however, they shared responsibility for framing and presenting an issue with the participants. Even though the session organizers were experts, they purposely "did not go first," meaning they contributed their viewpoints organically during the course of a dialogue. Organizers actively sought dissenting or alternative views. The format was not only popular, it proved effective at producing practical action strategies. In short, the product was not an elegant and eloquent presentation, but a dialogue that produced deeper understanding and ideas for action (for a more detailed description, see *No Better Time*, 2010, p.16). We recommend that the academy study and experiment with this learning exchange model for classroom teaching, public forums, and collaboratively organized public problem solving. In doing so, campuses should draw from the work of communities and civic organizations and employ study circles, issue forums, world cafes, "fish bowl" exercises, and other approaches to model democratic processes.

Today's students are increasingly driving a shift toward more use of electronic forms of public engagement. The 2008 presidential election proved how powerful social networking and electronic communication can be for drawing young people into the ebb and flow of a campaign. Today, rather than relying on clubs and student leaders, students self-organize activities (including protests) through Facebook. Most students get their news through the Internet. Universities need to experiment with electronic media to raise awareness about issues and encourage public problem solving.

#5: Model Democracy

Educating for democracy also means "being the change" that we would like to see in the world. It is all well and good to call for democratic renewal, but as our institutions continue to disproportionately serve a privileged constituency, our actions will speak far louder than our words.

We are a nation of many cultures, yet we are also intensely segregated. Many students arrive at college from largely homogeneous communities. Nearly a third (31 percent) of incoming first-year students in 2009 said that they had not socialized with someone of another racial or ethnic group during the past year (Higher Education Research Institute, 2010). We cannot thrive as a democracy if we do not have a rich understanding of American diversity and the socioeconomic and historical realities that shape our lives.

In 2009, the American Council on Education issued its report on who completes high school, who attends what kind of institution, and who attains a degree. Over the past twenty years, college enrollment rates have increased, and currently 41 percent of the traditional college-aged population is enrolled in college. Despite this overall progress, racial and ethnic disparities not only exist, they are growing slightly because of disproportionate rates of improvement. Asian Americans have had the highest rate of enrollment (63 percent), followed by white students (from 31 percent in 1988 to 45 percent in 2007), African Americans (from 22 percent to 33 percent) and Hispanics (from 17 percent to 27 percent) (Ryu, 2009).

Rates of college attainment among first-generation students, low-income students, and students of color are significantly lower than those of their peers (Lumina Foundation, 2009). Only 7 percent of high school sophomores whose families are in the bottom quarter of the income distribution complete four years of college, compared to 60 percent of those from the top quarter (Dynarski and Scott-Clayton, 2008). Testifying before Congress in 2008, researcher Susan Dynarski reported, "Even among the smartest kids, income is a strong predictor of college attendance."

Nor are students from different demographic groups experiencing education equally. Attending schools with higher student-average SAT Reasoning Test scores, higher tuition, and other measures of college "quality" correlate positively to a higher probability of graduating, postcollege earnings, and acceptance to graduate schools (Espanshade and Radford, 2009, p. 16). Low-income students, first-generation college students, and students of color disproportionately attend colleges that lack the resources of the elite schools.

The people teaching at the most-selective institutions are disproportionately white and male and prospects for change are not encouraging. A 2009 report by the American Council on Education (based on 2007 data) notes that among more-junior, tenure track faculty members at four-year institutions, only 5 percent are women, and only 4 percent are people of color. The numbers are only slightly better for community colleges, 6 percent for both categories (Hartley, Eckel, and King, 2009, pp. 22–23).

Institutional leadership is similarly disproportionate. People of color hold 16 percent of senior leadership positions and 14 percent of the presidencies (Hartley, Eckel, and King, 2009, p. 32). The numbers are better for women: 23 percent of college presidents and 45 percent of senior administrators are women. Stated another way, 86 percent of the presidents are white and 77 percent are male, facts that are hard to swallow when males represent half and whites represent 68 percent of the overall population.

These questions of equity in higher education (and others such as the treatment of adjunct faculty, gender and racial disparities, and benefits for same-sex couples) call for action of the kind proposed in this book—campus and community dialogues designed to generate change in institutional structures, processes, and decisions. The dialogues need to happen on individual campuses, not just at annual academic conferences, and campuses need to ask, what can happen here, on this campus, to interrupt these patterns?

Another place to start is locally, with an examination of where pockets of poverty exist and how individual institutions can change the patterns described here. Campuses can work to close local and regional disparities, particularly in educational achievement.

There is a profound disconnect between civic and diversity initiatives on campuses. It is a shame because many of the people championing such efforts share the same deep commitment to creating a more just society. Questions of race and our democracy are inextricably linked. As Cornel West eloquently puts it, "The fight for democracy has ever been one against the oppressive and racist corruptions of empire. To focus solely on electoral politics as the site of democratic life is myopic" (West, 2004, p. 15). People championing democratic engagement and diversity need to actively seek one another out to build strong coalitions that can produce meaningful change.

Conclusion

Democracy is not simply a form of government; it is a way of living. Democracies are strong when societal norms impel citizens with different interests and attitudes to live and work together and tackle pressing public problems. It was this very characteristic—the inclination of everyday people to share this responsibility rather than to appeal to some central power (a monarch or government official)—that captured Alexis de Tocqueville's ([1835, 1840] 1969) imagination when he visited America in the early nineteenth century.

Democracy is fragile and ephemeral. It must be reborn and nurtured by each generation. Deliberative democracy—this generation's promising vision for a strong democracy—reflects a recommitment to the fundamental democratic values that de Tocqueville saw expressed nearly two centuries ago. It is an expansive call for everyday citizens from diverse social, economic, and political perspectives to participate in public problem solving for the benefit of mutually common good.

In a fully realized deliberative democracy, all free citizens would have an equal opportunity to participate in the social, political, and economic systems that affect their lives. This ideal requires more egalitarian conditions than currently exist in American society. For this reason, deliberative processes must purposefully include an examination of underlying patterns of power and privilege if they are to be legitimate. Dissenting views must not only be tolerated, but purposefully sought out and considered. Further, as the founders of our political system understood, values dilemmas lay at the heart of society's most pressing problems and different priorities and values among the citizenry must be recognized and addressed in the political process to avoid the tyranny of the majority and a reversion into polarized factions.

Academic freedom, the robust exchange of ideas, free, intellectual inquiry, imaginative critique and problem solving, the pursuit of knowledge, courage, tolerance—these are cornerstones of higher education. They must never, however, be viewed as ends in and of themselves. Rather, they are matters of deep interest and value to American democracy.

What makes deliberative democracy so appealing is that it holds equal promise for democratic renewal and students' learning. Its principles—inclusion, reason, neutrality, respect, and collegiality—can also guide the academy toward more democratic dialogue and political deliberation about the problems facing our communities, our nation, and the world, more examination of the values tensions that public problems engender, and more learning about how to improve people's lives, build communities, and strengthen democracy.

References

de Tocquville, A. *Democracy in America*. Garden City, N.Y.: Doubleday, [1835, 1840] 1969.

Delli Carpini, M. X., and Keeter, S. *What Americans Know about Politics and Why It Matters*. New Haven, Conn.: Yale University Press, 1997.

Dynarski, S. Oral testimony before the Subcommittee on Select Revenue Measures House Committee on Ways and Means, May 1, 2008. Accessed February 20, 2010, from http://www.brookings.edu/~/media/Files/Projects/hamilton/testimony/0501_educa tion_tax_incentives_dynarski.pdf.

Dynarski, S., and Scott-Clayton, J. "Complexity and Targeting in Federal Student Aid: A Quantitative Analysis." National Bureau of Economic Research Working Paper 13801. Cambridge, Mass.: National Bureau of Economic Research, 2008.

Espenshade, T., and Radford, A. W. *No Longer Separate, Not Yet Equal: Race and Class in Elite College Admission and Campus Life*. Princeton, N.J.: Princeton University Press, 2009.

Hartley, M., Eckel, P. D., and King, J. E. *Looking beyond the Numbers: The Leadership Implications of Shifting Student, Faculty, and Administrator Demographics*. Washington, D.C.: American Council on Education, 2009.

Heierbacher, S. *NCDD's Engagement Streams Framework*. Boiling Springs, Penn.: National Coalition for Dialogue and Deliberation. Retrieved July 22, 2010, from http://www.thataway.org/exchange/files/docs/ddStreams1-08.pdf.

Higher Education Research Institute. "The American Freshman: National Norms Fall 2009." Los Angeles: Higher Education Research Institute, University of California Los Angeles, 2010. Retrieved July 22, 2010, from http://www.heri.ucla.edu/PDFs/pubs/briefs/brief-pr012110-09FreshmanNorms.pdf.

Lane, E. "America 101." *Democracy Journal*, 2008, *10*, 53–63.

Lumina Foundation. *A Stronger Nation through Higher Education, 2008*. Indianapolis: Lumina Foundation. Retrieved January 4, 2010, from http://www.luminafounda tion.org/publications/A_stronger_nation_through_higher_education.pdf.

No Better Time. "No Better Time: A 2010 Report on Opportunities and Challenges for Deliberative Democracy." Durham: The University of New Hampshire, The Democracy Imperative, 2010. Retrieved July 22, 2010, from http://www.unh.edu/demo cracy/pdf/NBTReport_1.pdf.

Public Agenda. "Americans Proud of U.S. and Constitution, but Want Children Taught the Bad with the Good." Washington, D.C.: Public Agenda, September 17, 2002. Retrieved July 12, 2010, from http://www.publicagenda.org/press-releases/americans-proud-us-and-constitution-want-children-taught-bad-good.

Ryu, M. "Minorities in Higher Education 2009 Supplement." Washington, D.C.: American Council on Education. Retrieved July 12, 2010, from http://www.acenet.edu/AM/Template.cfm?Section=CAREE&Template=/CM/ContentDisplay.cfm&ContentID=34214.

West, C. *Democracy Matters.* New York: Penguin Press, 2004.

Wichowsky, A. (with Levine, P.). "What Young People Know." College Park, Md.: The National Alliance for Civic Education, 2002. Retrieved July 6, 2010, from http://www.cived.net/wypk.html.

NANCY L. THOMAS *directs the Democracy Imperative at the University of New Hampshire and is a senior associate at Everyday Democracy.*

MATTHEW HARTLEY *is associate professor of Education at the University of Pennsylvania.*

NEW DIRECTIONS FOR HIGHER EDUCATION • DOI: 10.1002/he

ADDITIONAL RESOURCES

America*Speaks*
http://americaspeaks.org/

The Center for Information & Research on Civic Learning
and Engagement (CIRCLE)
http://www.civicyouth.org/

Deliberative Democracy Consortium
http://www.deliberative-democracy.net/

The Democracy Imperative
http://www.unh.edu/democracy/

Everyday Democracy
http://www.everyday-democracy.org/

Kettering Foundation
http://www.kettering.org/

National Coalition for Dialogue and Deliberation
http://www.thataway.org/

National Issues Forums
http://www.nifi.org/

Policy Consensus Initiative
http://www.policyconsensus.org/

Public Agenda
http://www.publicagenda.org/

Public Conversations Project
http://www.publicconversations.org/

New Directions for Higher Education, no. 152, Winter 2010 © Wiley Periodicals, Inc.
Published online in Wiley Online Library (wileyonlinelibrary.com) • DOI: 10.1002/

INDEX